The Philosophy of John Locke

Twenty-four of the most important
publications on Locke's philosophy
reprinted in sixteen volumes

Edited by
Peter A. Schouls
The University of Alberta

A GARLAND SERIES

Some Thoughts Concerning the Several Causes and Occasions of Atheism

Socinianism Unmask'd

John Edwards

Garland Publishing, Inc.
New York & London
1984

BT
1100
.E3
1984

For a complete list of the titles in this series
see the final pages of this volume.

These facsimiles have been made from copies in
The British Library.

Library of Congress Cataloging in Publication Data

Edwards, John, 1637–1716.
Some thoughts concerning the several causes and
occasions of atheism ; Socinianism unmask'd.

(The Philosophy of John Locke)
Reprint (1st work). Originally published: London :
J. Robinson, 1695.
Reprint (2nd work). Originally published: London :
J. Robinson, 1696.
1. Apologetics—17th century. 2. Atheism—
Controversial literature. 3. Socinianism—Controversial
literature. 4. Locke, John, 1632–1704. I. Edwards,
John, 1637–1716. Socinianism unmask'd. 1984.
II. Edwards, John, 1637–1716. Socinianism unmasked. 1984.
III. Title. IV. Series.
BT1100.E3   1984   211'.8   83-48568
ISBN 0-8240-5603-5 (alk. paper)

The volumes in this series are printed on
acid-free, 250-year-life paper.

Printed in the United States of America

SOME
THOUGHTS
Concerning the Several
Caufes *and* Occafions
O F
A THEISM,
Efpecially in the
Present Age.

With fome Brief Reflections on
SOCINIANISM: And on
a Late BOOK

Entituled

The Reafonablenefs of Chriftianity as deliver'd in the Scriptures.

BY

JOHN EDWARDS, B. D. and fometime Fellow of S. *John*'s College in *Cambridge*.

LONDON: Printed for *J. Robinfon* at the *Golden Lyon*, and *J. Wyat* at the *Rofe* in S. *Paul*'s Churchyard M DC XC V.

TO THE

Most Reverend Father in GOD,

His GRACE

THOMAS,

By Divine Providence

Lord Archbishop of *Canterbury*, Primate and Metropolitan of all *England*, &c.

MY LORD,

YOUR Grace being not only by Your Place and Station, but by Your own Choice and voluntary Act, the *Grand Patron of our Religion*, it cannot be improper to present You with these brief Papers, which, though

A 3 in

The Epistle Dedicatory.

in themselves very mean and inconsiderable, and unworthy of Your Grace's View, are a Vindication of that *Holy Cause* against the repeated Cavils and bold Insults of *Atheistical* Spirits, who (as Your Grace with a very deep Resentment and Regret * observes) are of late grown very numerous. How vigorously Your Lordship hath attacked this sort of Men, is well known to the World; and that hitherto they have not been able to bring about their impious Designs, is in great part owing to Your Lord-

---
* Sermon of the Folly of Atheism. Sermon at the Queen's Funeral.

ship's

The Epistle Dedicatory.

ship's succesful Attempts. I presume, from the Encouragement which so Illustrious an Example hath given me, to engage in the same Cause, that is, to lay open the *Folly* and *Absurdity* of their Pretences, and withall to discover some of those Heads and Springs whence the Atheistick Apprehensions of these present Times arise, and whereby they are fed and nourished. Which I hope will be of good use to those who desire to be caution'd against the Venom of this Raging Evil, and will in some measure operate even on those who are infected and

A 4   cor-

The Epistle Dedicatory.

corrupted with it already.

I am sensible how Precious Your *Grace*'s Minutes are in this time of extraordinary Business and Emergency; and therefore I will not be injurious to the Publick by any farther Applications to Your Grace. Only I superadd my hearty Prayers for Your Health and long Life, wherein the Common Welfare and Happiness both of Church and State are so much involved: And so I subscribe my self,

Your Grace's
Most Dutiful Son,
and Devoted Servant,

John Edwards.

THE
PREFACE.

I Designing, by the Divine Help and Conduct, to defend the Existence and Providence of God by Arguments drawn both from the Greater and the Lesser World; it is my Request to the Reader, that he would accept of this Brief Essay *in the mean time, which I conceive will be a suitable Introduction and Preparative to that other Undertaking.* For as in that intended Discourse I shall carefully trace and discover the Footsteps of the Divinity every where; so here I make it my Business to shew how frequent and obvious the Occasions of Disbelieving it are. By which means we shall effectually learn how to purge our Minds of those ill Qualities which naturally are subservient to Atheism; we shall know how to remove those Stumbling-blocks, to answer those Objections, and to clear up those Mistakes which usually betray Men to this Infidelity. And thus there will be a
Way

The PREFACE.

Way made for what I design. Persons will be fitted to receive and retain the Impressions which those Topicks that I shall afterwards make choice of will enstamp upon their Minds: And I hope the Age, which hath lately been stigmatized with Marks of Atheism, will for the future be renowned for those truly illustrious and glorious Characters.

I will only farther acquaint the Reader, that some part of what I here offer (viz. such Particulars as I thought were convenient for an usual and mix'd Auditory) was deliver'd lately in one of the City-Pulpits; and the other Heads, with their Enlargement (which are of somewhat a different strain, and are chiefly adapted to the Curious and Inquisitive) are an Addition since. But as I have added several things, so I have omitted some, at the Desire of those who are concern'd in both. This is all that I had to advertise the Reader of; and so I bid him

Farewel.

SOME

SOME
THOUGHTS
Concerning the
Causes and Occasions
OF
ATHEISM.

THAT the World was not void of *Atheists* in King *David*'s time, may be gathered from his Words in *Psalm* xiv. 1. *The Fool hath said in his heart, There is no God.* But it is exceedingly to be lamented, that the number of them is much increased since, yea, that it is the Unhappiness of this Present Age, to be pester'd with

Some Thoughts concerning

with not a few of them. Notwithstanding those cogent and incontestable Arguments for a Deity which are suggested from the Holy Scriptures, and the Natural Reasonings of sober Minds, there is still an *Atheistical* Spirit prevailing in the World. There is a sort of Men (if I may call *them* so whose bold Infidelity is so Irrational and Brutish) that reckon the Notion of a *God* to be a Melancholick Conceit, and the mere Effect of Credulity and Ignorance. Yea, there are some that pass for *Wits*, who strive for the honour of being accounted the most *Able Atheists* of the Age.

Wherefore, instead of rehearsing or urging those Topicks which are wont to be produced for the Proof of the *Divinity*; my Business at present shall be, to enquire into the *Causes of Atheism*, which now vaunts it self with an impudent Fore-head,
and

and begins to boast that it hath got Footing in a great part of the World.

I will search into the *Occasions*, either real or pretended (for I will mention both) of this Reigning Mischief. I will shew you on what *Grounds* the Impious do at this Day not only, with the Psalmist's *Atheistical Fool, say in their Hearts,* but openly and avowedly proclaim to the World, that *there is no God*, that is, no Supreme Over-ruling Being of infinite Perfection, no eternally Wise, Intelligent, and Omniscient Substance that at first gave Existence to all things, and ever since upholds them, and takes care of them.

I. I assign *Ignorance* to be one great Spring of this gross Unbelief. As *knowing* as the World is at this day, there are too many People of inferiour Rank whose Education hath been so unhappy, that they
have

have not been instructed in the Common Principles of Religion; and they are more unhappy in that they will not allow themselves time and leisure to look into their own Minds, and to rouze those inbred Notions which are implanted there by God, and which would (if they would give way) lead them to him. Wherefore it is the Concern of all Persons, to know how to converse with Themselves, and to rifle their own Breasts, that they may find a *Deity* written there: and besides, they should be careful to acquire such a stock of Knowledge from without, that they may understand their Religion, and not be seduc'd by Atheistical Notions that fly up and down every where.

But this first Cause which I assign of *Atheism*, is not only to be found in some meaner sort of People who have not time (as they order their Affairs) to think of a God, but in others of a higher Rank and Quality: for by *Ignorance* I mean a wilful and sottish stifling of natural Notions and Impressions: And this sometimes prevails in Men of great Parts and Knowledge.

Think it not strange that I reckon such Persons in the number of the *Ignorant*; for (to speak impartially) they are so: and this was the Sense of the * wisest *Pagans* long since. For to have no Knowledge, and to stifle it, is the same thing; which is the Case of these Men: they make it their business to choak the innate Principles of their Minds, and to disregard those Notices which their Natures suggest to them. Thus these Persons are stubbornly and obstinately ignorant. Whatever their Pretences and Boa-

---

* Ἀνόητον ἀνάγκη κỳ ἄθεον ᾗ, κỳ τ̃ ἄθεον ἀνόητον. Hierocl.

stings

stings be, their Atheism proceeds from want of Learning and Wit. For 'tis not the part of a Learned and Ingenious Man to destroy the Notions of Mankind, and pull down what hath been built by the universal Suffrage of the World, and in its place to erect a Conceit of his own. Some may take such for Brainish and Scholar-like sort of Men, but then these are so without *Thinking*; for it is the want of this that makes them what they are. Or, to say the best of this kind of Men, an *Atheist* is but a *half-witted* Person: He hath perhaps made some Attempts in Science, but to little purpose: He hath attain'd to some slight and trivial Notions, but hath not penetrated into the heart of Things; and thence it comes to pass, that he is full of Doubts and Cavils, which he is able to raise, but he hath not Skill and

and Ability enough to answer them. Wherefore it was excellently said of my Lord *Bacon*, * *A little Philosophy inclines mens minds to Atheism;* but depth in Philosophy brings mens minds about to Religion and a Deity. Thus though this misshapen Monster would be thought to be the genuine issue of True Wisdom and Sound Knowledge, yet it is really the daughter of an Affected Ignorance. Wherefore to secure your selves against Atheism, be careful that you blind not your minds; willingly receive the rays of light into your souls, cherish all sound notions and conceptions, and by all proper methods bring your selves to a right understanding, and steady embracing of all the Fundamental Principles of your Religion.

II. There is great *Disingenuity* and *unhandsome Dealing* in the case,

* His Essays.

else we should not have so much *Atheism.* Here I will prove, that they do not act fairly, but that they are *Ungenteel,* which perhaps will affect these Persons more than any thing that I can say. What they are willing and forward to grant in other matters, and on other occasions, they refuse to grant here, yea they utterly deny it, though there be the same reason for one as the other. This plainly appears by their *Objections.*

As first, they tell us they have no Sensible Notices of a God, and therefore they can't admit of it; for all the knowledge (say they) which we have of things, is deriv'd to us from Sense. But here we see that these Men are *Partial* and *Disingenuous,* for they will not deny that there are many things which they judge not of by Sense; they grant that the swiftness of Motion often-

the Causes of Atheism.

oftentimes out-runs the nimblest Sense, and the Observation of the quickest eye; yet they do not deny the Motion it self: The Element of *Air*, in which they daily converse, is not seen, nor is it heard or felt (unless when 'tis extraordinarily moved and disturbed, which is but seldom:) nor will they say they taste it; and 'tis as certain that they cannot smell it, (for this is only the Vehicle of Smells, but is not it self the object of that sense) and yet these nice Gentlemen do not deny the Existence of the *Air*. They can by none of their Senses discern the Motion of the *Sun*, *Moon*, and *Stars* (or, as perhaps they think it most proper to say, the Earth), and yet there is not a man of them that denies that they move. It can't be determin'd by Sense, whether the Sun be bigger than it appears to be, and therefore

fore *Epicurus* (who was a great Man for Sense) held it was of no greater dimension than it seems to the Eye to be; yea, of no greater heat in it self than it seems to the Feeling to be here on Earth. And the Atheistical Poet, who borrow'd his Notions from him, was of the same mind,

> *Nec nimio solis major rota, nec minor ardor*
> *Esse potest nostris quàm sensibus esse videtur.*
> Lucret. lib. 5.

This is certain, that the things that are least discernible act most. The Animal Spirits, which do all the great things in our bodies, are themselves Imperceptible. They are the Insensible and Invisible Parts, as Spirits, Wind, Subtile matter, Exhalations, which (being agitated) do the chiefest Exploits in Nature. There are Fine Particles and Atoms diffused through all bodies whatsoever; and these are the cause of Sense

the Causes of Atheism.

Sense and Motion in Animals: by help of these, Minerals, Plants, and all Vegetables, are brought to perfection. These Invisible Agents effect strange things, and act most wonderfully in the World. The *Nutritious Juyce* in the Nerves, if we may credit the famous *Glisson*, is of mighty use and influence: yet (as he confesses himself) there are no Cavities to be seen to convey it, and none of this *Succus* is ever discern'd in the dissecting of Animals. Notwithstanding this, some Physicians of the most piercing Judgment, have granted (whatever they do now) the real being of it. And in other Instances it might be shewed, that *Sense* is not always made a Judge even in sensible Objects, but we gather the being and operation of them from Reason and Discourse. This the persons whom we are now dealing with do not deny, but even practise

practise it themselves, and are willing to allow of it. Why therefore are they so void of Ingenuity and fair-dealing, as not to admit of the same in the case that is before us? Why do they most irrationally deny a God because they do not apprehend him by Bodily sense, whenas they judge not of some other things by Sense, nay though they be proper objects of it? This is a plain proof of these mens wilful Prejudice and Partiality, especially if I add, that *God* is infinitely farther removed from our most exalted Apprehensions, than the *Sun* (of which we spoke before) is from this Earth. This Glorious Sun * *dwelleth in that light which no man can approach unto, whom no man hath seen, or can see.*

Secondly, they tell us that there are *Great Difficulties* in conceiving a

---
* 1 Tim. 6. 15.

the Causes of Atheism.

God, and they are loth to swallow these down: and more especially the notion of a *Spirit*, i. e. a Being that is void of Matter and Body is too hard to be conceiv'd by them, and therefore seeing we hold *God* to be a *Spirit*, they can form no conception of him. I will reply to both the parts of this Objection distinctly: and first as to the General Cavil, That this notion is accompanied with *Difficulties*, I answer, there are great Difficulties in other matters, which yet they leap over with ease, and do not disbelieve the things themselves because of the Difficulties that attend them. It is very hard to explain how a little Wheel of two inches diameter, fixed on the same Axil with two greater Wheels of ten inches a-piece, moving together (the greater ones on the ground, the lesser on a table) should move over the very same space

space in equal time, with equal rotation with the greater ones: and yet the thing it self is not denied by any one. And many other puzzling Problems might be mentioned, where the Hardship doth not discourage them from embracing them. But I will instance in one of their own Hypotheses, *viz.* that of *Atoms*, which they chuse to solve the Original of the World by, that they may evade the *insuperable Difficulties* (as they think them) of the Acknowledgment of a *God*. If they say that these Atoms had their Existence from *Themselves*, then instead of denying one God, they assert many, for Self-existence is of the very nature and essence of a Deity; wherefore if they were all from themselves, they are all *Gods*. If they say that *other* Matter or Atoms were the first Cause of these, then they run to Infinity, and no body is able to trace them. If they say they are of *Nothing*, then they had as good have begun with that, and have confessed in plain terms, that the World was made out of Nothing, and then they come to us, but they are resolved they will not do that. Thus they are confounded as to the *Rise* and *Origine* of their Atoms.

Then, as to their *Motion*, whence had they that? either of themselves or of an other? They could not have it of *Themselves*, for we see it is not of the nature of Matter to move: it is in it self a dull and inert, a lumpish and unactive thing. If this Motion was impress'd on it by an *Other*, then that was either some *other Matter*, or *something else*. If they hold the former, they run again *in infinitum*, and he is a distracted man that will run after them. If they maintain the latter, they

they betray their Cause, and acknowledge a *Spirit*, for there is no real and substantial thing besides Matter and Spirit. In brief, whether the former or the latter Assertion be held by them, they do in a manner own what they deny; for we will not disagree about the Name, if we can agree on the Thing it self. That Being or Agent which gave the first Motion to things, is *God*.

If after all they say, that Matter had this Motion by *Chance*, and so was neither from it self or any other, they talk more absurdly and wildly than before; for *Chance* is a Word made to signifie only the *unexpected happening of a thing*, but doth not import that there was no Cause or Author at all of it. But however, if they will stand to this (as generally they do) that Matter at first had a strong power by *Chance* to jump into an Orderly System

the Causes of Atheism. 17
ſtem of *Heavens,* *Earth,* *Sea,* &c.
then I ask them, What is the reaſon that there hath been nothing of this nature ſince? What reaſon can be given why all the Atoms and Effluviums in the ſeveral Ages and Succeſſions of Time, ever ſince this viſible World had its being, have not produced ſome excellent Frame either like this World, or of an other nature? What! is this *Lucky Chance* quite ceas'd? Is this *Fortunate Lottery* at an end? Is there no probability of a brave fortuitous hit once again? Is there no ſuch fine piece of work as that of *Sun,* *Moon,* and *Stars,* to be expected once more? No: there is an utter deſpair of it; for from Eternity (according to them) to this moment, we have had no ſuch good Luck, and therefore what reaſon have we to expect any ſuch afterwards? yea indeed, what ground have theſe
Chance-

Chance-Philosophers to think that there ever was any such thing? What reason have they to declare it to be their firm perswasion that Matter was set into motion from Eternity, and that by the frisking of its Particles, it at last danced into a World? yet this and all the rest they believe and vouch rather than they will hold that the beginning of things was from an *Intelligent* and *Wise Being*.

It appears hence, that they will say any thing rather than acknowledge themselves to be in the wrong: they make nothing of talking idly and impertinently, of running into Banter and Nonsense, as we have heard. They can give credit to this extravagant Fancy, that an everlasting Juncto of *Atoms* did without Counsel and Knowledge club together to make the World. They can tamely submit

to

the Causes of Atheism.

to this unaccountable Maxim, that these infinite Bodies, after eternal Brushings, Agitations, Encounters, Knockings, Tiltings, Justlings, Jumblings, fell by mere Chance into this excellent Frame that we now behold. Thus the Atheist, to avoid some seeming Difficulties, runs into those which are really so, yea into the greatest Absurdities imaginable. If it be difficult to conceive the Self-existence and Eternity of one God, surely it is insuperably so, to conceive infinite Matter moving it self, and giving Being to it self from all Eternity. It is plain then, that these men deal not fairly and uprightly, but wilfully deceive themselves and others. They cry up Reason, and yet maintain things which are repugnant to ordinary Discourse and the Common Dictates of Reason; and therefore are rather to be exploded than with much

much industry to be confuted. They cannot only swallow down, but digest *Absurdities* when they think fit, and at other times they can fancy them where there are none, nor any shadow of any.

Then as to that particular Difficulty, *viz.* That the Notion of a *Spirit* is inconceivable, and therefore they have no conception of a *God*; I return this brief Answer, That if this which they say be true, if it be impossible to apprehend the Idea of a *Spirit*, then there is no such thing: and if so, then *Matter alone* must do all things in the World, but particularly, it must have *Understanding* and *Knowledge*, it must *think* and *reason*, for (whatever the precarious Hypothesis of Atoms suggests) the Curious frame of this World could not be erected without Knowledge and Wisdom, and it cannot be kept up and managed

naged without these. Now, I appeal to any considerate man, whether the flat denying of this, and the asserting that the *Dimensions of a Body* are *Intellectual*, that to be *Long* and to be *Broad*, and to be *Deep*, are Acts and Exertments of *Reason* or *Will*, and (in short) that *Extension* is *Thinking*, be not far greater Absurdities than any thing they imagine to be in the notion of a God. It is a sign therefore that these men make Difficulties where there are none, and do not take notice of them where they are. I could here prove that our Faculties may form as clear, explicit, and distinct an Idea of a *Spirit* (which they so much boggle and startle at) as they do of their own Existence, or any other Principle in Nature; but this I have made my task in another place.

Thirdly,

Thirdly, they tell us they cannot believe a Deity, becaufe there are no Proper *Demonftrations* to prove it. For you muft know, that thefe Perfons whom we have to do with at prefent, are great men for *Demonftrations*. But I anfwer, The Exiftence of many things in the World cannot be made out by *Demouftration*, ftrictly fo called, and yet no man queftions the reality of them. The skilfulleft Mathematician under Heaven can't demonftrate that the Sun fhines, and yet there is no doubt at all of it, and he would be counted a Mad-man that denies it. We are morally certain of many things which we cannot poffibly demonftrate; but this doth not hinder us from yielding a firm affent to them. And 'tis certain, that an Affent is as firm on Moral grounds as on rigid Demonftrations, when the matter is capable

ble of no other grounds; for the Evidence is proportionable to the Matter to be proved, and that is as much as can be desired by any intelligent man. There can be no greater than a Moral Certainty of a Deity: for there are no grounds of it Mathematically Demonstrative. But by being Morally Certain we are certain enough, and as certain as the nature of the thing will bear. This should content any Rational man, and it is unreasonable to demand any more.

Then, as for those *Demonstrations* which they talk so much of, they cannot but acknowledge, that as they are sometimes managed they yield but little Certainty. For, not to speak now of the old *Academicks* and *Scepticks*, who denied *Geometrical Principles*; or of *Demetrius, Sextus Empiricus, Epicurus, Zeno,* and others of the Ancient Philosophers who reason'd against them, I will mention some of our *Moderns* (and those of great Skill and Learning) who have disagreed about Mathematical Proofs, and thereby proclaim to the World their Uncertainty. The greatest Astrologers hugely differ as to the distance of the Sun from the Earth. It is nearer to it ten thousand miles than it was, saith *Copernicus*. But *J. Scaliger* would have the Writings of those Authors who hold the Sun is nearer to the Earth than 'twas in former days, * *to be razed out with sponges, or the Writers themselves to be corrected with stripes.* And other very good Astronomers are so far from consenting to this, that they maintain the Sun is farther off from the Earth than it was at first. And yet on both sides they proceed on *Mathematical* grounds. There is no

---

* Exercitat. 99.

the Causes of Atheism.

Mathematical Demonstration for *Comets* being above or below the Moon, saith * *Ricciolus,* a very skilful Mathematician: but others of that Faculty have pretended much to the contrary. The *Paralax* is well known to be a Mathematical business, that by which the Planets are judged to be higher or lower: but the greatest Astronomers have quarrell'd with one another about this Doctrine. *Tycho* is for it; but *Claramontius* is against it; and *Galilæus* even *explodes* the Proof brought from the *Paralax.* Dr. *Wallis* and Mr. *Hobbes*'s Contrasts in Print, shew that *Mathematicks* are dubious: and this latter (who was so stiff an Opposer of the Notion of a *Spirit,* and consequently of a Deity) finds fault with all Geometricians, old and new, in his Book entituled *The Principles and*

---
* De Cometis.

Ratiocination of Geometricians. *Cartes's Dioptricks* and *Geometry* are pretended to be baffled by other Learned Mathematicians, as *Bourdin*, *Hobbes*, *Fermat. Franciscus du Laurens*, and Dr. *Wallis*, scuffle about a Mathematical Problem. So that it seems it is not an Infallible Science. *I am certain,* saith * Dr. *Henry More, that Mathematical Certitude it self is not absolute.* There is an *Essay* of Dr. *Pell* to shew the Errors and Mistakes of the best and most celebrated Astronomers for want of better Knowledge in *Geometry*. Even † Monsieur *Malebranch*, a profound Admirer and Follower of *Descartes*, acknowledges that in his *Geometry there are some footsteps of the weakness of the humane mind.* And I will conclude with the Words of One that was known to be eminent

---

* Preface before his Philosoph. Writings. † Search after Truth, Book 3. Chap. 4.

the Causes of Atheism.

in Mathematical Studies, * *Even in Geometry and Arithmetick* (saith he) *how many things are forcibly concluded to be true which are inexplicable, unimaginable, incomprehensible?*

Thus you see the Mathematical Certainty which some men talk of, is not so easily to be attain'd as they fancy. Disputes have place in *Geometry*; *Demonstrations* sometimes prove to be *Paralogisms*. But as for a Mathematical Demonstration for the proof of a GOD, it is vainly and unreasonably required, because there can be no such thing, for the matter will not bear it. Wherefore though † some *Divines* have been great *Philosophers* and *Mathematicians*, yet they never attempted any such thing. A man

---

* Bishop *Ward's* Serm. † Copernicus, Lansbergius, Clavius, Petavius, Tacquet, Scheiner, Gassendus, Fromondus, Kircher, Ricciolus, Oughtred, Ward, Wallis, More, Glanvil.

must not expect to have every thing proved the same way. If we have things evidenced by the Arguments which they are capable of, it is satisfactory, and every wise man rests in it. And these men themselves do so in other things: they acquiesce in that Evidence which the things admit of, and they seek no farther. Which shews, that in the present Case they are *Disingenuous*, and *Cross-grain'd*, and act merely out of Prejudice; which was the thing I undertook to make good. Their *Insincerity* nourishes their *Atheism*. Therefore let us have a care that we give way to no such thing.

III. Another Cause of this Pernicious Opinion, is, *Ostentation of Wit*. For you may take notice, that this Mischievous Plant springs from Contrary Seeds. As before this kind of men put on a very grave and solid Countenance, so now they

they shew themselves to be very Pleasant and Airy, and set up for the Art of Drolling. Before they appear'd like Philosophers, now they come upon the Stage like Buffoons. Then with a Magisterial Grimace they affected Demonstrations; now nothing will please them but the Comical part. It is observable, that they are a sort of Jesting, Scoffing People, giving themselves to Railery and Burlesque. And it is this Jocular Humour that in part betrays them to *Atheism*, for they take liberty to jest with their Maker. These witty and facetious Folks must needs play with Heaven, and laugh God out of his being. They are defective in sound Learning and Judgment, and in the place of these have a fanciful way of Jeering, which they addict themselves immoderately to. *Democritus* was the great

great Asserter of Eternal Matter, and thought that the Casual Motion of it was the Cause of all things: the influence of which Principle on his Cogitations, made him at last laugh at every thing he saw, and mock at all Actions and Occurrences of humane life; for 'tis certain that if they are all by Chance, they are to be denied. The Followers of this Great Man have learnt from him to be *Laughing Philosophers*; and there are abundance of this Sect now-a-days. This I look upon as one Cause of the great *Atheism* of this Age. They think *their Tongues are their own*, and they may say what they please; and they perswade themselves, that what is wittily said is well said. Hence these Sparks venture to ridicule Religion, to scoff at Virtue and Piety, and to mock God himself. Then at last they really believe what they fancy'd, fancy'd, and jestingly utter'd; and they assert in good earnest what at first perhaps was said only in Merriment. Wherefore, to guard your selves from *Atheism*, be always very Serious, and abhor the sportful vein, the flashy fancy of these men, who think they can't be men of Parts unless they make a mock of God and Religion. Whereas the Brightest and most Accomplish'd Heads ever exploded this: and in our own Nation we have abundant Instances of this, that even the * Wisest and the Wittiest Men (tho no Church-men or Divines) have express'd their deep sense of *God* and serving him, and defied the contrary Profane *Atheistical* humour.

IV. *Pride* and *Self-conceit* may justly be reckon'd another Spring

---

* *Sir* Tho. More. *Sir* Phil. Sidney, *Sir* W. Raleigh, *Sir* Hen. Wotton, *Lord* Bacon, *Mr.* Selden, *Mr.* Cowley, *&c.*

of Atheism. Men in this and former Ages have thought it below them to go tamely along with the generality of Mankind in asserting a Deity. They would be thought wiser than others: and consequently they affect to go against a commonly receiv'd Notion. But more particularly these High-Flyers account it base and sneaking to listen to an Old Story of *Religion*, and to submit their Belief to *the Harangues of the Parsons*, as they are pleas'd to word it. Especially *Great Men* are apt to be possessed with this Pride, and consequently to be Atheistical. They strongly incline to King *Alphonsus*'s impious Bravado, *That if he had been present at the Creation, he would have framed the World better than 'tis now.* There is in many an excessive Desire of a Name and Vogue; and they think to obtain them by scorning the Common way,

the Causes of Atheism.

way, and going out of the beaten road, by giving the Lye to all Mankind. And though one would think that they might shew the subtilty of their Wit by diving farther into things than the Vulgar, and not by casting off the agreed Sentiments of Mankind; by refining and improving the Principles of Nature, and not by nulling and evacuating them; yet they choose the latter, that they may (as they think) give the greater proof of their Wit and Parts, and that it may be seen that they are able to weather a Cause be it never so bad. To maintain this all sober Considerations are postpon'd; they superciliously renounce (when they are in the Humour) all Reason and Arguments; they arrogantly resolve to hold the Conclusion, whatever becomes of the poor Premises. *Atheism* owes its Being much to this,

this, as I apprehend; as I think it it is sufficiently evident from what I have said before, when I shew'd that they chuse rather to maintain the greatest Absurdities, than to adhere to a Received Truth. Wherefore that we may effectually prevent this Folly in our selves, let us banish Presumption, Confidence, and Self Conceit; let us extirpate all Pride and Arrogance; let us not lift our selves in the number of Capricious Opiniatours.

V. *Undue Apprehensions* of a Deity joyn'd with *Superstition* are the high road to Atheism. Those that think amiss of God will easily be enclined to question his Existence. It is too true that men model the Divinity according to their own fancies: the Creature fashions his Creator. Or, like him that engraved his own Image in that of the Goddess, they shape themselves and
figure

figure out their own abfurd notions and conceits, whileft they pretend to give the Pourtraiture of God. Therefore impofing of falfe Doctrines concerning the *Attributes* of God is very pernicious, for they are deftructive of his very being and nature. It is no wonder that when thefe come to be fcann'd and examined, men doubt of the very exiftence of God, becaufe fo irrational and abfurd things are attributed to him. They are loth to think there is fuch a One, or they wifh there were not. So that they endeavour to deftroy that which they can't endure. Thus miftakes and mifprifions concerning God lead to Atheifm. Falfe Conceptions of a Deity expunge at laft the belief of one.

And fo 'twas of old in Paganifm, *Idolatry* was the great mother of *Atheifm*: grofs *Superftition* undermined

mined the Godhead. It hath been falsly and blasphemously said that * *Fear* was it which first introduced a God into the world: but yet it is certainly true that This with some persons hath expelled the notion of him out of the world: for they being Timerous and Melancholick create to themselves strange fancies concerning Him whom they are to worship, and represent him to their thoughts as Severe and Tyrannical. And the *Gentile* Priests and Rulers laid hold on this passion of *Fear*, and did what they could to promote and heighten it, that thereby they might keep the people in awe. To which purpose they invented Innumerable Rites and Ceremonies, many of which were harsh, troublesom and afflictive. So that Bigotry and Excess in Religion made way for none at all: and when they were

---

* Primus in orbe Deos fecit timor. —— *Pap. Stat.*

wearied

the Causes of Atheism.

wearied with the intolerable burden of it they cried out, with that Nonsensical Atheist,

Tantum Religio potuit suadere malorum.

Then Religion it self and the Author of it were discarded. This was caused by the *Undue Representations* which were made of God: the Priests would have the Superstitious Bigots believe that the *Divine Numen* could not be appeased without those wild Observances. This is that which *Plutarch* took notice of, telling us that * from such gross, absurd and extravagant Devotion men came to disregard a Deity, and to conclude there is None rather than to believe there can be Such a one, one that is delighted with so unaccountable Ceremonies and Usages. Therefore, to shut out Atheism, let us have right concepti-

---
* Περὶ Δεισιδαιμονίας.

ons of the Supreme Being whom we worſhip and ſerve. It concerns us to aſſert *rightly* the notion of God, leſt otherwiſe we ſlide into a disbelief of any. Who miſrepreſenteth the Divine Being is in a ready way to deny him.

VI. *Corrupt Affections* and *Lives* (for I will joyn both theſe together, becauſe they are never aſunder) make men *Atheiſts*. Men of depraved minds and manners doubt of all Religion becauſe they Like none, and at laſt they flatly deny what they Love not. An Atheiſt firſt deſires and wiſhes no God, and his deſires and wiſhes work on his Underſtanding. His Willingneſs to have it ſo enclines him to believe it. He eaſily credits what he longs for: his Affection corrupts his Judgment. Thus the indulging of Luſt and Vice diſpoſe a man to Atheiſm. To which purpoſe obſerve the Soil where this

Poiſon-

Poisonous Weed springs up, grows, and thrives most, *viz.* in the Courts of Debauch'd Princes, among such Nobility and Gentry, and in Great Cities where vicious and prophane living is most in fashion. They are lewd and dissolute in their manners, and give themselves up wholly to the satisfying of their Lusts: and this naturally prejudices them against the belief of a God and a life to come. Nothing doth so much extinguish all apprehensions of these as Carnal Pleasures. He that lives dissolutely and wickedly can't easily entertain the notion of a God, for 'tis counter to his course of Living. Therefore he goes on in his Debauchery, and huffs and swaggers, and perhaps swears by the Divinity that there is none. It is plain that this sort of men decry a God, because they would not be obliged by his Laws. Sensuality makes them desirous to remove all stops of a wicked life, and therefore they whet their wits (such as they are) to annihilate Religion, and to extirpate a Deity. An abhorrence of the Practical part of Piety engages them against the Theory. Their Lives influence on their Belief. They are addicted to Atheism by their Lewd and Prophane Courses.

For we must observe this, that these two mutually advance one another. As Atheism is the highway to Wickedness (which the Psalmist takes notice of when he saith, *The fool hath said in his heart, There is no God: Corrupt are they, and have done abominable iniquity*, Psal. 53. 1.) so 'tis as true that Wickedness is the original of Atheism and Infidelity. For 'twas rightly said by a Great Man, * *None deny there is a God but*

---
* Lord *Bacon*'s Essay of Atheism.

those

those for whom it maketh that there were no God. For they know that if there be one, he will certainly judg them for their evil doings. They cannot therefore be secure in their sins unless the notion and remembrance of a Deity be blotted out. It is their supposed Interest then, not their Reason, that makes them deny a God; for it is their Concern to be perswaded, that there is none to punish them. Briefly, they are unwilling to believe any thing but what their Lust shall put into their Creed. Thus you see the true Reason of the Atheism of these times. It is fed and pamper'd by Luxury; the constant Fumes and Steams of this affect the Brain, and discompose the Intellect. Practical Atheism leads to that which is Dogmatical, *i. e.* holding and believing that there is no God. Evil and perverse minds, profane and debauch'd lives, strangely byafs and incline men to this. Wherefore if you would effectually shut out this Vile Perfwafion, take care to fupprefs your Evil Affections and Practices, for thefe are wont to court mens underftandings to turn Atheifts.

VII. Atheifts take occafion from our *Divifions*, *Broils*, and *Animofities*, from the many *Parties* and Squadrons of *Sects* that are in the World, to bid defiance to all Religion; and they refolve to profefs none till they can fee them all Agreed. Thus * *Tully* obferved of old, that the Diffentions of Philofophers, the various Sentiments and Opinions that prevail'd among them were a caufe of fome mens denying a Deity, at leaft of their ftaggering about it. And truly this Obfervator himfelf, in his Books *De Natura Deorum*, is fo given to the *Aca-*

---

* De Nat. Deorum, Lib. 1.

demical

demical vein of Disputing, that he seems sometimes to be irresolv'd whether there is any God or no. So it hath been among some of those who have taken upon them the external Denomination of *Christians*. The Differences in Opinion, the Errors and Heresies which they take notice of, cause them to suspect yea to renounce all Truth. A great deal of the Atheism of this present Age may be ascrib'd to this. Some behold the great Scufflings that are about Religion, not only the Single Combates, but the Pitch'd Battels that are about it, and thereupon they discard all thoughts of any such thing, and become perfect Libertines. And herein they are promoted and push'd on by such persons as the Author of *Fiat Lux* and the *Treatise of Humane Reason*, who both design *Scepticism*, and so *Atheism*.

But though it is thus, though the Different Perswasions about Religious Matters have this ill effect, yet this can be no true Reason why any man should renounce the Belief of a God. For he that is truly rational and considerate, will rather make this an Argument of the contrary: for it was foretold by * Christ and his † Apostles, that Errors and Delusions should be in the World, and therefore the *Fulfilling* of these Prophecies be as witness not only to the Truth of the Writings of the New Testament, and consequently of Christianity, but of the Divinity it self. For things of this nature, which depend wholly on free and arbitrary Causes, cannot be foretold without Divine and Supernatural help. None but an All-seeing eye could have a prospect of

---

* Mat. ~. 15. Luke 17. 1.   † 1 Tim. 4. 1.   2 Tim. 3. 1, 6.   2 Pet. 3. 3.   Jude 18.

these future Occurrences. The Predicting of such things to come is an Evidence of an Omniscient Deity.

And then as to the thing it self, why should any man think it Strange and Unaccountable that there are *Dissentions* in Christendom? He may as well wonder that there are *Men* in the World; for as long as these retain their nature, *i. e.* are subject to Prejudice, Love of Interest, Passion, Pride, and the like, there will be *Errors* and *Heresies*, for these proceed from some of those ill Principles: and unless God should change the frame of the World, and destroy the freedom of Man's will, *i. e.* make him another Creature, it cannot be otherwise. How unreasonably then do men question a God, and cry out against Religion it self because they see so many of this sort of Disorders

ders in the world? Whereas it is certain, that it is not the fault of Religion that things are thus, but they are thus because men have so little Religion.

Again, the Cheats and Delusions that are in the world are useful for the *Trial* of Mankind, *that* (as the Apostle saith) *they who are approved may be made manifest,* 1 Cor. 11. 19. I do not say they were *design'd* for this (for no Evil is design'd by God) yet it is certain they are expedient for this purpose; and there is no better way to have an experiment of the Upright Judgment, Sincerity, Faithfulness, and Constancy of Persons, than by their being expos'd to these Impostures. Lastly, God deservedly *Punishes* men with erroneous and false Doctrines. 2 *Thess.* 2. 10, 11. *Because they receive not the love of the truth (* yea because they hate it, and oppose themselves to

the Causes of Atheism.

to it *) and have pleasure in unrighteousness,* for this cause he sends them strong delusion, that they shall believe a Lye, and that they shall defend and maintain it. It is just with God to leave men to the Error and Blindness of their Minds, and judicially to give them over to Atheistical Perswasions when they have wilfully debauch'd and abused their Faculties. This is the dreadful, but just Judgment of God; and I doubt not but the present *Atheism* of this Age is such.

Thus it is evident that Errors and Dissentions about Religion are so far from being Arguments of the Non-Existence of a Deity, that they are undeniable Proofs of it. Let not then the diversity of Sects and the Disputes of wrangling Heads (as particularly the late upstart Contract between the *Unitarians* and *Trinitarians*) prejudice us

against

against our Christian Faith. But let us rather be stirr'd up hence to hold fast the Principles of our Belief, and to own a Deity when there are so many in this degenerate Age that deny it. And withal, let us endeavour to banish *Atheism* by doing so to our *Divisions:* let us lay aside our Religious Squabbles, and arrive at last to a happy Agreement in Doctrine, that we may hereby cut off occasion of Atheistick Unbelief on this Account. However, though in some Points we can't fully accord, let us not be hot and firy against one another, as if Charity were no Virtue with us.

VIII. There is something more heinous than *Divisions*, which frequently occasions Atheism, and confirms men in it; and that is, the *Hypocrisie* and *Evil Practices of too many that make a very fair profession of Christianity.* Whilst it is observ'd

the Causes of Atheism.

serv'd that they talk Religiously, and pretend to Holiness, but *do* nothing of what they talk of or pretend to; whilst it is seen that they have *a form of godliness, but deny the power thereof*; whilst it is evident that they cry *the Temple of the Lord, the Temple of the Lord*, and yet are unhallowed in their Lives; whilst it is known that they lay claim to the Spirit, but are Carnal and Sensual in their Manners, and enterprize very vile things for their worldly Profit and Advantage; in short, whilst it is observ'd that the Behaviour of sundry of the avowed Professors of Christianity is unanswerable to their Principles, there is a sort of men that for the sake of these, presently conclude all to be Hypocrites, and Christianity it self to be an Imposture. This then I grant, that the Unbecoming Lives of Christians are an *unhappy occasion*

of

of Atheism sometimes, but they can never be alledged as a *sufficient one*. For what though there be mere Pretenders to *Godliness*? doth it thence follow that there is none at all? What though there are great numbers of Religious Impostors? Must I therefore thence conclude that all Professors of Religion are an errant Cheat? Then by the same Logick I may peremptorily infer, that there is no such Metal as *Silver*, because by too noted experience we find at this day that it is generally counterfeited; and there is no such thing as True Coin, because so much is adulterated amongst us. No man of sense will make these Conclusions: and 'tis as certain, that he can with as little reason make the others. Let us not then be abused by unsound and fallacious Inferences: let us not think there is no Religion be-

because

cause there are so many Unworthy Retainers to it. Yea, let us be fully convinced of this, that though Christianity hath been, and is to this day abused and sophisticated, and thereby dishonoured; yet it is a Reality, and we may venture our Lives upon it. And seeing the Evil Deportment of some that profess Christianity is the greatest encouragement to Atheism and Vice, let us all make it our great business to adorn our Profession with a holy, strict, and exemplary Conversation. Let our *light so shine before men, that others seeing our good works* may be so far from denying, that *they may glorifie God.* And let us pray for the arrival of that Happy Day (and I hope it is not very far off) when Religion shall universally bear sway upon Earth, and when men shall be throughly convinced of the real Worth of Christianity

ſtianity from the Practices of thoſe that profeſs it.

IX. In the next place, more particularly, the *Ill Examples* of ſome who by their Office are *Spiritual Guides and Inſtructors*, are mention'd as another great occaſion of Irreligion and Atheiſm. It is neceſſary to take notice of this, becauſe it is alledged (but very frequently without ground) by the ſworn Patrons of that Cauſe which I am now pleading againſt. They obſerve of ſome of this Order of men, that they urge Virtue and Holineſs with great Warmth and pathetick Zeal, and yet are very cold, yea wholly neglectful in the Practice of them, and viſibly favour thoſe Vices and Enormities which they diſſwade others from: whence it is no wonder (ſay they) that theſe Perſons are not believed to be in good earneſt, yea that they are

the Causes of Atheism. 53

are thought not to believe themselves, *i. e.* to be really perswaded that those things are true which they discourse of; for it is seen, that their Lives wholly contradict their Doctrine. Whence this rash Conclusion is made, that Preaching is a meer Trade, that the Ministerial Function is a Cheat, and that Religion it self is so too, and that a Deity is no other. Thus where is there more of *Atheism* than in *Italy*, the Pope's own Soil, part of which is call'd *Holy Land* ? Which the Observing * Author of *Europæ Speculum* (who had convers'd in his Travels with the *Italians*, and knew them very well) attributes to the gross Wickedness of the *Roman Clergy*, and particularly of the Popes and Cardinals, of whose scandalous Speeches and Actions the people of that Country have a greater

---
* *Sir* Edwyn Sandys.

know-

knowledge than others. They are not ignorant that several Popes were inclined to be Atheists; as *Paul* 3. when he was dying told the Standers! that he should now know three things; *viz.* whether the Soul be immortal, whether there be a Hell, and whether there be a God. And *John* 23. (as is plain from that Council of *Constance* by whom he was deposed) profess'd that he look'd upon Religion as a Fable, and God and the Soul's Immortality as such. And they dayly behold the lewd and dissolute Practices of some of the Cardinals and Prelates, Abbots, Monks, and of their Parish-Priests, which very thing (as the foresaid Author observes) makes them the most Irreligious People in the World, yea causes them to defie *all Religion* for their sakes. Especially they conclude, that there is nothing true and real in *Christi-*
anity,

anity, becaufe fo many of the eminent Pretenders to it and Affertors of it, live continually in oppofition to all Religious Principles and Practices, and are feen to be guilty of the moft horrid Impieties, of the moft execrable Villanies that are to be imagined. Their being fo near to the *Head of that Religion* (as he is ftiled) makes them averfe to the whole kind. And this is *in fome meafure* the cafe of People in other Countreys, where even the *Proteftant* Faith is profeffed, but is accompanied with the Scandalous Lives and Lewd Practices of fome that are immediately concern'd in Holy things, and whofe Employment it is to direct others in Religion.

But to fpeak impartially to any confiderate Perfon, this cannot yield an occafion of being *Atheiftical:* for though the manners of *fome* of the

Sacred Function be offensive, yet 'tis irrational and absurd to blast all Religion for their Misdemeanours. We do not read that our Saviour condemned the *Jewish Church* and *Mosaick Law* because of the Hypocrisie and Wickedness of the Chief Priests, Scribes, and Doctors of the Law. Nay, he tells the People, *All that they bid you observe, that observe and do; but do not ye after their works,* Matth. 23. 3. As much as if he had said, The Moral Law, and all the Offices of Religion, are not in the least discredited by the vicious Manners of some of your Teachers. Be careful that you imitate them not in their Practices; but be very observant of the Holy Doctrine which they deliver; entertain no ill Thoughts of it, because of the corrupt Lives of your Guides. The like may be said now; the Faults and Miscarriages

riages of any Ecclefiaftical Perfons muft not be charged on the Sacred Inftitution of Chrift; we ought not to think ill of Chriftianity for the diforderly Behaviour of any fpiritual Officers in the Church. We fee that there is no man refufes to follow a Learned Phyfician's Prefcriptions and Rules concerning Health, becaufe he doth not obferve them himfelf. Nor can the Spiritual Patient with any reafon reject the Rules of Saving Health and Happinefs, though they are not obferv'd by the Prefcriber himfelf.

But to be yet more plain with the Perfons I am now dealing with, *they* (of all men) cannot with any tolerable pretence make ufe of this Plea: they cannot complain of the Lives of the Clergy as adminiftring to their difregard of Religion, for the more ftrict and religious any Church-man is, the more is he defpifed spised and hated by them. A Pious Clergy-man is reckon'd by them a weak shallow Creature, a fantastick Bigot, and is laugh'd at as such. So that it is evident, that what they alledge concerning the undue Behaviour of some that serve at the Altar, is a more groundless Cavil; for they would have all men as Wicked and Debauch'd as themselves.

It must indeed be acknowledged, that this is a great Scandal, and of very pernicious consequence, and such as is not to be permitted with impunity in the Church: but it is no excusable ground of Impiety and Atheism. However, since it is so heinous in it self, and is made by the perverse minds of many an Excuse for their Atheism, it is the concern of all Christian Guides of Souls to be Examples to the Flock, to conform their Lives with great Circumspection and Exactness to the Laws of Christ Jesus their Master, and to take care to perform themselves whatever they require others to do.

X. Unbelief of a God is occasion'd sometimes by the *Strange Revolutions* and *Changes*, the *Odd Events*, and *Unaccountable Administrations* that are in the World. Especially men are inclined to question God's Existence as well as his Providence when they behold the prosperous state of the most vicious Persons, and on the contrary, observe how miserably sometimes the Best men are treated in this Life, and at Death are not at all differenc'd from the Worst, but perish alike. Then you shall hear one cry out, *Quis putet esse Deos?* And another uses the like Language of the Poet,

Dum rapiant mala fata bonos,---
Sollicitor nullos esse putare Deos.

But any underſtanding man, who will take time to conſider and deliberate, will ſee that nothing of this nature can juſtly adminiſter matter of Atheiſm. For it muſt be remembred, that we are finite ſhallow Creatures, and are not able to comprehend the Wiſe Deſigns and Purpoſes of Heaven in every Event that we ſee: and therefore when we meet with obſcure and rugged Diſpenſations, and ſuch as ſeem to be very diſorder'd and irregular, we have no reaſon to find fault with them, and to think them unworthy of God, and of Divine Providence, becauſe we are not able to make a judgment of them. Thoſe Events which ſeem to be excentrick and at random, are guided by a ſteady unerring hand: but we have not depth of Apprehenſion to conceive it at preſent. But it may be afterwards, when our minds are more enlightned,

the Causes of Atheism.

ned, we shall know how to solve these difficult *Phænomena*. However, at the last Day all these Intrigues, these Knots, these Labyrinths, these Riddles, shall be fully resolved; and it shall be part of our employment in the other world, to admire and adore the Infinite Wisdom of God in the disposal of the Affairs here on Earth. And particularly we shall then be satisfied, yea we may be now, concerning the foresaid Problem, *viz.* the Prosperity of the *Wicked*, and the contrary Circumstances of the *Good*; for 'tis evident, that these are according to exact Justice and Wisdom. God intended the former should *have their portion in this life only*; and he designed the latter to be prepared for Heaven by those rougher dealings here below.

Lastly, *Learned Times*, especially if accompanied with *Peace* or *rity*, are reckon'd by a * Judicious Person as another Cause of Atheism. Nor is this inconsistent with what I said before, that *Ignorance* is the Mother of *Atheism*. For Learned or Peaceable times are only thus far conducible to this Great Evil, that men are then generally too Inquisitive and Curious, too Nice and Wanton, and over-busily pry into Secrets; which when they cannot satisfie themselves about, they are inclined to be Atheistical, and to doubt even concerning the chief things of Religion. Wherefore I question not but the starting and keeping up at this day the Debates about the Doctrine of the *Holy Trinity* are a great advancement to this evil disposition of mind. There are those who push on both Parties to wrangle and quarrel about this Grand Point, and in the

---
* Lord *Bacon's* Essays.

mean

the Causes of Atheism.

mean time laugh at the Combatants on both sides. Whilst they encourage some Writers to baffle the *Trinity of Divine Persons*, their Project is to destroy the *Essence it self*. Whilst they put them upon maintaining the Unity of the Godhead, they hope in the close of the Dispute to introduce a Nullity not only of the Deity, but of all Religion. For by these Bandyings backward and forward, they know that mens minds will be unsettled and that they will be apt to waver about the truth and certainty of the main Articles of our Religion. When Persons observe, that the very Divinity of our Blessed Lord and Saviour is toss'd and torn by rude Pens; when they see so *Catholick* a Doctrine attack'd with such Violence; what can they think of the other great Verities of Christianity? And withall, the *Anti-Trinitarians*

nitarians hereby provoke some of their *Adversaries* to an indecent sort of Language concerning these Holy Mysteries: so that some of these latter have hurt the Cause it may be almost as much by their Defending it, as the others have by their Opposing it. Thus it must needs be when Persons immoderately indulge *Curiosity* in these Abstruse and Sublime Matters, and will not be content with what the *Bible* and *immediate Inferences* drawn thence suggest to us. By this means they lose their hold, and give their Antagonists a clear Advantage against them, and manifestly promote the Design of those who make it their work to make void the Notion of a Deity.

Nay, in the very *Socinian* Doctrine it self there seems to be an *Atheistick* Tang. Would not a man guess that there is an approach to Atheism

the Causes of Atheism.   65

Atheism in those Reflections which are made on a Sermon preach'd by the Right Reverend Bishop of *Worcester,* * where one of the most receiv'd Notions concerning the Nature of the Deity it self is cashier'd. The *Self-Existence* of God, which is the Primary, Fundamental, and Essential Property, and is the very Life and Soul of the explicatory part of the Doctrine of the Deity, is peremptorily pronounced by them to be a *Contradiction.* It is well known, *Socinus,* and *Crellius,* and others of this Party, deny God's *Immensity,* i. e. his being present every where as to his Essence and Nature. All of them agree, that he hath not a Knowledge and Foresight of every thing that happens in the World, for future Contingencies are hid from him. Particularly

---
* Considerations on the Explications of the Doctrine of the Trinity, *Page* 5, 6, 7.

Socinus

* *Socinus* largely argues against this *Præscience,* and tells us, that he is to be laugh'd at that asserts the contrary. Nay, it is farther observable, that this great Patriarch of the present Cause disowns the *Immaterial* or *Spiritual Nature* of God, as may be undeniably gather'd from his † Exposition of *John* 4. 24. and other Passages in his Writings. And he is followed by *Crellius,* as is manifest from that Account which this latter gives of a *Spirit,* when ‖ he speaks of the Nature of God. He doth not make it to be any thing above a *refined body, a substance void of all gross matter,* such as the Air or *Æther* is. So that when these men call God a *Spirit,* their meaning is, that he is a Fine and Te-

---

* *Prælect.* cap. 8, 9, 10, 11.   † *Fragment. Disp. de Adorat. Christi.*   ‖ *Deus est Spiritus æternus: spiritum autem cum nominamus, substantiam intelligimus ab omni crassitie, qualem in corporibus oculorum arbitrio subjectis cernimus, alienam. Hoc sensu Angelos dicimus Spiritus, & Aerem,* &c. *De Deo & Attrib.* cap. 15.

nuious

nuious fort of Matter, not that he is wholly Incorporeal, and altogether free from Matter. This is the fame with Mr. *Hobbs's* Corporeal God. Thus four of the Chief Attributes of the Deity, viz. *Self-Existence, Omnipresence, Omniscience,* and *Spirituality,* are either in whole or in part rejected. Whereupon, I ask this Queſtion, Whether theſe things do not diſcover a Tendency (to ſay no more) in the *Anti-Trinitarians* to that which I am charging them with? For to aſſert a God, and yet to deny ſome of his Choiceſt Properties (whereby we know him to be God) is in effect the ſame with denying a Deity.

If they diſtinguiſh between the *Engliſh* and *Foreign Socinians* (as I perceive they do) and tell us that the former do not aſſert the things before mention'd, I anſwer, the very *Engliſh Prints* avouch the firſt
of

of those Particulars: and as for the rest, they being the Doctrine of the *Chief Patrons* of the Socinian Cause, yea and of the *Most* of *them*, the English Unitarians are involved in them, because those Foreigners are the greatest and most substantial part of that Body of men call'd *Socinians*. Thus the *Trinitarian Scheme of Religion*, drawn up by some English Socinians of late is thought by them to touch all the Trinitarians (else it could not be stiled the *Trinitarian Scheme*) though every individual Trinitarian doth not hold all those things mentioned there. Let them apply this, and they will have nothing to object.

And further, I would argue from their own avowed Principle, which is that *they are to admit of nothing but what is exactly adjusted to Nature's and Reason's Light, nothing but what is entirely clear and evident*:

for

for though it is true some Socinian Writers of late have laid aside this Notion (and truly we may observe that they are shifting every day their Arguments, and so we know not where to have them) yet he that is acquainted with the Writings that make up the main Body of Socinianism knows full well that this is a Principle constantly asserted and maintain'd by the generality of them, and upon all occasions insisted upon. This hath been the Stanch Notion of the Great Dons of the Party, and of the famous *Socinus* himself. And *Slicktingius*, though he seems indeed sometimes to be otherwise perswaded, yet comes to this at last, that the *Trinity* is a Doctrine that *can't be borne*, because *it can't be understood*. And why do * *Crellius* and others argue from Rea-

---

* Comment. Vol. I. page 118. † De Uno Deo P. lib. 1. sect. 1, 2.

son and Logical Arguments againſt the Trinity, if they do not refuſe the Doctrine upon the account of Reaſon? And it is certain they would not do this if they were not perſwaded that theſe things in Religion muſt be adjuſted to Natural Reaſon, and that they are diſpleaſed with the Doctrine of the *Trinity* and *Incarnation*, &c. becauſe theſe are not exactly ſquared to their Natural Notions. You ſee then what is the ſentiment of the Greateſt Rabbies of this way, and therefore we muſt make our eſtimate of the Socinian or Antitrinitarian Doctrine from theſe, and not from one or two Modern Writers. This I think will be granted by all men of reaſon.

But what if it doth appear that even the very *Engliſh* and *Modern Socinians*, though they ſeem to wave this Principle, do yet retain it, and govern

govern themselves by it? Else why do they complain that * *they have no conception of the Trinity* as the Trinitarians represent it to them, *they cannot form an idea of it; it is a notion that excites no idea's in their minds; it is against Reason and Natural Light?* We are advised by the *Modern* Penmen † *to consult our Reason about the thing in question; and if we do so, we shall find an absolute impossibility in the Trinitarian Doctrine: our Reason will assure us that an Almighty Father and an Almighty Son are most certainly two Gods, and that two Creators can be no other than two Gods: therefore we may, and we must infer that the explication of the first Verses of St.* John's *Gospel, which advances such a Doctrine, is certainly false.* Again, the *English Socinians* tells us that ‖ *the*

---

* Letter of Resolution concerning the Doctrine of the Trinity. The Unreasonableness of the Doctrine of the Trinity. † An Accurate Examination of the Principal Texts, &c. chap. 5. ‖ Observations on the Answer to the brief History of the Unitarians, chap. 2.

Some Thoughts concerning

Doctrine of the Trinity clashing altogether with our natural idea's can be no matter of Revelation, and therefore ought not to be believ'd. And hear their Final and Resolute Determination, which fully speaks their absolute adherence to this Principle, † *We abide by this Argument, here we fix our foot, never to be removed, that the inconsistence of the Trinity (as well as the Incarnation) with Reason and Natural Knowledge being undeniably evident, therefore this Doctrine can have no real foundation in Divine Revelation, that is to say, in Holy Scripture.* And we find that our *English Unitarians* * argue from *Reason* in this Point, and they declare that they cannot believe it because Reason doth not teach it. Thus we find that the bottom of all is, the Trinity and such like Doctrines are

---
† Letter of Resolution concerning the Doctrine of the Trinity. * Observations on the Answer to the brief History of the Unitarians, chap. 1.

above

above their Reason, and Natural Idea's, and therefore they are no matter of their Faith. This is it which the Reverend Person before named charges these men with in a great part of his * Sermon: and certainly he would not have done it if there were no such persons in being. It is too plain that there are such, and I think I have proved it from their own mouths. The sum of their Opinion and resolution is this, that there is nothing difficult and abstruse in Religion, and that they will not believe any thing in Christianity but what they can make out by Reason: otherwise it must be discarded presently.

* Of the Mysteries of the Christian Faith.

Now, to apply this Principle of the Antitrinitarians; we are assured that *we cannot by searching find out God*, Job 11. 7. his *Infinite Nature and*

and *Immense Essence* are not commensurate to our Conceptions, are not adjusted to our Idea's, but are far above them: it is impossible that the Apprehensions of finite Creatures should reach these things: therefore according to the foresaid Principle, the *Unitarians* are not obliged to believe any such things; they must not admit of the Infinite Nature of God, concerning which our Conceptions will always be obscure and unproportionate; yea, they cannot but infer from their own Maxim, that *God* is an impossible Being, at least that His *Immense Nature* is such. They cannot comprehend and conceive the Manner of the Immense and Infinite Presence or Knowledge of God; therefore they must disown the things themselves. Thus by vertue of their own profess'd Principle, the *Godhead* it self as well as the *Trinity*

Trinity is shock'd by them: and consequently one would be apt to gather that a *Socinian*, so far as he is led by this Principle, is an *Atheist*, or (lest that should seem harsh) one that favours the Cause of Atheism. For he may as well quit the belief of a *God* because of these Difficulties and Abstrusities in the Nature of God, as renounce the Doctrine of the *Trinity*, because there are some inexplicable and unintelligible things that accompany it. But because all men do not follow the natural Conduct of their Principles (the Divine Providence over-ruling in these cases) I do not here pass an Universal Censure, I do not speak of every individual man, nay I hope charitably concerning most of them. However, it is to be fear'd, that some are unhappily under the force and sway of the foregoing Principle; and these

these are the Persons I speak of, and no other.

These things I freely and openly suggest. Which the Learned and Ingenious Gentlemen of the *Racovian* Perswasion cannot dislike, unless they disapprove of themselves, unless they disclaim their own Writings; for they cry up in almost all of them (and in * one very lately) a Freedom of Discourse, a Liberty of speaking their Thoughts, which they applaud as a very *Generous* and *Noble* thing, and much value themselves upon it. They cannot deny that to me which they allow of and magnifie in themselves, especially when I most sacredly profess to them that I have sincerely delivered my Thoughts, and spoken what I conceive to be the words of Truth and Soberness. Wherefore I expect to be approved of by Persons

---
* An Exhortation to a Free and Impartial Enquiry, &c.

of their Ingenuity and Free Temper, who (as I find) blame others (even some of the Clergy) for palliating and dissembling, and not speaking out. I think they will not charge me with this Fault, for I have acted according to their own Generous Principles: and I must tell them there is not a Friend of theirs in all their dear *Eleutheropolis* that is more disingaged and unbyass'd than I am.

But though I have used a becoming Freedom, yet there are some things that I omit, because I would let the World see that I am not eager and lavish in blaming and censuring any Party of Men, especially since it is suggested to me by some that are Learned and Sober of that Perswasion, that it is hard that their Opinion should suffer for the *Ill Consequences* of it, or for the *Insincerity* of any that profess it, or by by reason of the *Rash indiscreet Passages* which occurr in some of their late Writers. I do it likewise because I would give the World an Example of Moderation and Temper in this Disputing and Wrangling Age; that it may be seen, that whilst I remonstrate against the Errors and Mistakes (as I suppose them to be) of any Side, I can forbear to publish the Aggravations of them, and that I had rather the Truth should prevail than the Contrary Opinion, or the Maintainers of it should be exposed. Finally, I consider that it is improper and unseasonable to contend among our selves at home whilst our Armies are engaging the Enemy abroad.

The Proper Antidote belonging to this Head of my Discourse is this; Let us make a Difference between *Finite* Beings and that which is

the Causes of Atheism. 79

is *Infinite*: for seeing there is such a Vast Difference between them, we ought to observe it. We cannot form the same Conceptions of one and the other; yea the latter is exalted above our reach and comprehension; wherefore let us be satisfied, that the Properties of an Infinite Being (such as *God* is) are incomprehensible, and therefore that may be possible in the Infinite Nature of God (as namely that it is communicable to Three Distinct Persons) which is impossible in the Finite Nature of Man or other Creatures. Let us attend to that which may be known, and that clearly and distinctly, and not trouble our thoughts and wrack our brains about Unsearchable Mysteries. A Lover of Peace as well as Truth should not be so much sollicitous about the *Manner of the Three Personalities or Subsistencies* as about
the

the *Trinity it self.* We are sure of the latter, as sure as the Scripture can make us; therefore it doth not become us to wrangle about the former; especially when we find that ill-minded men make use of this Quarrel to promote the Cause of Atheism; and truly they make advances towards it every day.

I proceed to Other Doctrines which administer to this Great Evil which I have been speaking of, and which may justly be reckoned among the Blemishes of these Inquisitive Times. Such is that of a * late Writer, that the Books of the Old Testament were not written by those Persons whose Names they bear, that the Historical parts of the Bible are lame and imperfect, and repugnant to themselves; that the Writings were not carefully and faithfully transmitted to us, but

---

* *Spinosa. Tract. Theol. Polit.* cap. 8, 9, 10.

abound with many faults and mistakes, that the Books of the *Prophets* are mere scraps and fragments, and taken without order and method from other Writings. All which put together, destroys the Authority of Divine Revelation, and consequently of all Reveal'd Religion, from whence we have the strongest and most pregnant Arguments for a Deity.

Again, The same Design is advanced in these *Learned Times* by thrusting of Opinions and *Theories* on the world in defiance of the plain *Letter* and *Historical Part* of the Bible: as if the Sacred History, which was written by Inspired Men, were not as credible and authentick as that of Prophane Authors. The frame of the *Primitive Earth* is represented opposite to what *Moses* tells us it was: the account which he gives of *Paradise*

(as it is a Particular Place) is contradicted, yea it is strongly averr'd, that there never was any such thing. What *Moses* relates concerning our *First Parents* is laugh'd at as a Romantick Story. The Universal *Deluge* in *Noah*'s time is attributed to an accidental diruption of the Earth; which when scann'd, is found to be fictitious and imaginary, and thence the Deluge it self is concluded by many to be so; and *Moses* is reckon'd by them as an Impostor. Which is taken notice of, and thus animadverted upon by a Curious Observer, and One who (as becometh so Learned an Head) joyns Religion with his Philosophical Researches, * *The Atheistical Party had hereby an occasion* (saith he) *boldly to give out that such a Deluge as that described by* Moses *was altogether incredible,*

---
* Dr. *Woodward*'s Hist. of the Earth, *Part* 3. 161.

and

and that there never was, nor could be any such thing. Nothing was talk'd of among them under Mathematical Demonſtrations of the falſhood of it, which they vented with all imaginable Triumph, and would needs have it that they had here ſprung a freſh and unanſwerable Argument againſt the Authentickneſs of the Moſaick Writings; which is indeed what they drive at, and a Point they very fain would gain. For if the Pen-man of the firſt book in the *Bible* be found tripping, then the Credit of all the reſt falls to the ground; we may juſtly queſtion their Fidelity, yea deny whatever they ſay. And ſo the *Bible* falls, and with it all our *Religion*, and with that neceſſarily a *Deity*, which is the thing ultimately aimed at, I do not ſay by the firſt Hand from whence theſe Notions came (for I charitably hope better things of ſo Learned a Perſon, eſpecially ſince
he

he hath shew'd himself not unwilling to retract them) but by those ill-minded men who make their Markets of these Opinions. All that I will add here is this, that if (according to a Learned * Doctor of the Sorbon) *it be a very dangerous Paradox to presume to deny that the Pentateuch was composed by Moses,* and accordingly *Hobbes* and *Spinosa* are condemn'd by him for using Arguments to that purpose, then surely it must be much more dangerous and pernicious to hold that any part of *Moses*'s Writings is mere Forgery and Fiction, *i. e.* was designed only to comply with the Ignorant *Jews* at that time, and doth not contain matter of fact. I have said something of this nature in another place, and on another account, but I never had occasion before to represent it as an unhappy Handle

---

* *Du-Pin* Hist. of Ecclef. Writers. *Prelim. Differtat.*

which Atheiſtically diſpoſed Perſons may lay hold upon. Wherefore let thoſe who are Philoſophically diſpoſed take warning hence, and forbear to prefer their own precarious Hypotheſes before the plain Account which this Inſpired Hiſtorian gives of thoſe firſt things in the World. Let none preſume to repreſent the Writings of this Firſt Author as falſe, in order to make their own true, and thereby to gratifie the worſt ſort of men. I need not ſay more here, becauſe I have already antidoted againſt the Infection of theſe two laſt Heads, *viz.* in thoſe Diſcourſes wherein I have treated of the *Authority and Perfection of the Scriptures.*

In the next place, Learned Enquirers are apt to give Encouragement to Atheiſm by *an obſtinate endeavouring to ſolve all the* Phœnomena *in the world by mere Natural and*
Cor-

Corporeal Causes, and by their averseness to admit of the aid and concurrence of a Supernatural or Immaterial Principle for the production of them. The *Mechanick Philosophy* hath done a great deal of mischief on this account: not but that (so far as it ought to be made use of) it is generally the most excellent (because the most plain and sensible) way of displaying the Operations of Natural Bodies: and it cannot be denied, that since This hath been revived and entertain'd, there hath been that Improvement in Natural Philosophy which never was thought of before, and which could never have been attain'd by the *Aristotelian* way: yet this is to be said with truth and reason, that the Great Reviver and Manager of it hath carried it on too far by undertaking to give an account of All Effects and Events in the production

ction of Vegetables and Animals, and in the very Formation and Organization of the Body of Man himself by mere Mechanick Principles, thereby in a manner ascribing Divinity to Matter and Motion. This Great Philosophick Wit over-shot himself here: and though it is true he hath otherways (*viz.* by asserting the Notion of *Souls* or *Spirits*, and by demonstrating the essential and real Difference from Bodies) made some part of amends for this, yet there are many at this day who make very ill use of this Doctrine. Some take occasion thence to believe, that Men as well as Brutes are no other than Engines and Machines, mere Neurospasts and Senseless Puppets. Others build upon this Notion the Conceit of *Thinking Matter*, for if *Pores* and *Particles* do all things in the

Bodies of Brutes, it is probable they serve instead of *Souls* to those of Humane Race: and so a Spiritual and Immaterial Principle is excluded. This *Philosophy* is *Vain Deceit*, and too many are *Spoil'd by it*.

But they should consider that the Noble French Philosopher himself did not believe all that he wrote. *Malebranch*, who was a great Admirer and Defender of him, tells us, that *he never pretended that things were made in that manner that he describes them* [*]. Yea, we have *Des Cartes*'s own word for it, [†] *I require not any one*, saith he, *to believe that Bodies which compose this visible World were ever produced in that way which I have represented them.* It seems by his own Con-

---
[*] Search after Truth, *Book* 1. [†] Princip. Philos. *Part* 4.

the Causes of Atheism. 89

feffion, that he was not in good earneft in all the parts of his Philofophy, and therefore we may gather that in fome of the Particulars aforemention'd he only propounded his Conjectures.

We might carry this Thought yet farther, and obferve that the generality of the Modern Philofophers (not only *Cartefians*, but others) have contributed much to Atheifm, by referring All things, not only in Organiz'd Bodies but in every part of the World, and all the *Phænomena* that we take notice of in it to a *Corporeal Principle*, and to the Efficiency and Power of this alone. Whereas, it is certain that there are many things which happen in the World that cannot be folv'd any other way than by the Superintendence of a *Spiritual Being*. There are feveral wonderful

Occurrences which no man can give an account of, but by supposing an Almighty Immaterial Agent, which is no other than *God*. Thus we must be constrained to repair to an Incorporeal Principle to solve the Cause of the *Seas constant Ebbing* and *Flowing*, and the *Attraction of the Loadstone*, and the *Hanging of the Clouds*, and many other *Phænomena* in Nature: for the Accounts that are given are imperfect and inconsistent, and do no ways satisfie any Serious Enquirer. A man that is not willing to be put off with slight and insufficient Suggestions, cannot rest in them as true Causes of those things. Only Philosophical men will be assigning some Reasons of things, whether they can or no: and this is an Inclination which is incident to the best and wisest Naturalists in all Ages. But

the Causes of Atheism. 91

But they may as reasonably undertake to shew whence it is that the Sun hath its continual Motion from East to West, or (as they would rather express it) why the Earth wheels about upon its Axis from West to East: which yet I do not see attempted by any Philosopher whatsoever; and yet there is as much reason for the one as the other.

So for *Gravity,* that known affection of Bodies whereby they are inclined towards the same Common Center, it seems not to be solved by any Principles of *Mechanism* that have hitherto been propounded, whether it be from a kind of *Magnetism* in some parts of the *Earth* (as hath been imagin'd by some) or from the reflected Particles of the *Celestial Matter* driving down into their places the earthy bodies they find above them, or (as they at other times are pleased to speak) from the *preſſure of the Atmoſphere*, which moves all Bodies continually downwards, becauſe it doth it ſelf preſs always towards the Earth: or whether it be (as the Learned *Iſaac Voſſius* holds) from the *Diurnal Motion of the Earth*, whereby all heavy Bodies (which move with greater difficulty than light ones) tend to the middle or Center, and light Bodies are expelled towards the Superficies or from the Center. But a man that would be very ſerious in Philoſophizing, can hardly acquieſce in any of theſe Solutions. He is not hereby ſatisfied how *Non-gravitation* can be and not be in a thing at the ſame time, as in Water in the Sea or in a River: for it is heavy and preſſes down, and yet the parts do not gravitate;

for

for 'tis known that those that dive, and are under so great a heap of Waters, yet feel it not upon them. Here must be Θεὸς ὑπὸ μηχανῆς, there must be acknowledged an other Cause besides those before mention'd (if they may be said to be *Causes* at all).

And accordingly I find that some of the most Judicious Philosophers of our own Nation have averr'd that a God, a Divine Incorporeal Substance may be evinced from the *Phænomena* of *Gravity*. This is made good by strong and nervous Arguments in an * Undertaking of the Learned Dr. *More*. † Another Ripe-witted Naturalist positively determines, that *the common Phœnomenon of Gravity is impossible to be explain'd by any natural operation of*

---
* Enchirid. Metaphys. Cap. 11.   † Mr. *Lock* concerning Education.

Matter, or any other law of Motion but the positive Will of a Superiour Being, so ordering it. And there is lately risen in our Horizon another Bright Philosophick Luminary, from whom we may expect Great Discoveries: it is his frank Acknowledgment that this wonderful Property of Bodies, whereby the World is tied and link'd together, and all things in it are kept from running back into their First Chaos and Confusion, and which consequently is necessary for the welfare, yea the very subsistence of the Universe, is supernatural. * *No power, saith he, of mere Nature can produce it: it surpasses all the Mechanism of Matter.* And in several other Instances which might be offer'd, there may be seen a despair of resolving the nature of them by material Causes wholly.

Dr. *Woodward*'s Nat. Hist. of the Earth. *Part* 1.

the Causes of Atheism.

No meaner a Person than * Doctor *Lower* (who was voted by all the Faculty to be one of the most Accomplish'd *Anatomists* of this Age) imputes the wonderful *Motion of the Heart*, and the *Circulation of the Blood*, to a Divine and Supernatural Cause. He who was as well skill'd as any man in the Fabrick of the Parts and Vessels of the Body, and knew all the Springs of their Actions and Operations, was of opinion, that these could not be solv'd by any ordinary Principle. I mention this only to let the Reader see that some of the Bravest and Wisest Philosophers are forward to own a Divine Hand even in the Common Works of Nature. They do not think it below a Man of Philosophy to resolve some things into an Immaterial Principle. For

---
* *De Corde.*

a Pious and Christian Philosopher may plainly discern that there are some things above the Efforts of Matter and Motion.

It cannot be denied (whatever some are pleas'd to say to the contrary) that we live in as *Learned Times* as ever have been extant. All Arts and Sciences are improved even to a Prodigy; and particularly the Accessions which are made to *Philosophy* are very great and astonishing. But yet I must needs concur with that very Thoughtful and Ingenious Gentleman before cited, who hath most truly told the World, that * *without the notion and allowance of Spirits our Philosophy will be lame and defective in one main part of it, when it leaves out the Contemplation of the most Excellent and Powerful part of the Crea-*

---
* Concerning Education.

tion,

the Causes of Atheism.

tion, viz. those Immaterial Beings. And herein he follows all the Great and Renowned Philosophers of our Age, especially those of our own Country, as Dr. *More,* Sir *Matthew Hale,* Dr. *Willis,* Mr. *Boyle,* Mr. *Ray,* &c. who pretend not to solve all things in Philosophy by mere Natural Causes, who look not upon Man as a piece of Clockwork, but have frequent recourse to those Springs and Causes which are Spiritual and Incorporeal, and sometimes to the immediate hand of the Almighty Himself. To conclude then, let not the inestimable Blessing of Knowledge and Learning which is so peculiar to this Age, make us forgetful of the Grand Source and Spring of all operations and effects in Nature. Let us beware of those men who ascribe all the Phænomena in the

the world to the power of the modified matter, and will leave nothing for God to do himself. Neither let us think that to Philosophize is to jar with the Sacred Writings, and to deny the very Natural History of it. The Scoffers at a Deity never had a more hopeful Harvest then since these Notions have prevail'd. By this means it comes to pass that *Philosophy*, which is the Study of Wisdom, affronts the Truest and Highest Wisdom; and even *Natural Philosophy*, which is one of the Choicest Accomplishments of humane minds, leads men even to the denial of the Author of Nature.

No wise man will disapprove of a Latitude either in *Philosophy*, or in the dubious and controverted Points of *Theology* : but then here he must be upon his guard, for there

there are those that under the pretence of throwing off some precarious things in the Old Philosophy, and discarding the empty Speculations of the Schools cast off those Principles which are useful and sound: under the notion of the Advancements of Arts and Sciences, and the Improvement of the *belles lettres*, and carrying Learning up to a greater heighth, they in the mean time help to pull these down. Especially in Religion, under the colour of searching further than others have done into Divine matters they abandon some of the choicest Principles: under the pretext of Reason and Good Sense they obtrude any New Conceit upon the world, and regard not the suffrage of the Holy Scriptures or of the Primitive Church. This they call a *Rational Religion*, and if
you

you offer any thing againſt it, they cry it down as a *Dream*, a *Romance*, a *Fable*, a *Phantom*, an *Hobgoblin*, and (which is a word which they think comprehends all the reſt) *Prieſt-craft*.

And here I might obſerve that among the Opinions which lead to Atheiſm, the denial of *Dæmons* and *Witches*, which * of late hath ſo much prevail'd, is none of the leaſt. For beſides that this is an open defiance to unqueſtionable Hiſtory, Experience and matter of Fact, and ſo introduces the worſt ſort of Scepticiſm (which is the high-way to Atheiſm) it is evident that this ſupplants the belief of *Spiritual Beings* or *Subſtances*: for Witchcraft and all Diabolick Tranſactions are disbeliev'd on the ac-

---

* Mr. *Hobbs* Leviath. chap. 34. Mr. *Webſters* Diſplay of ſuppoſed Witchcraft. Dr. *Becker*'s Enchanted World.

count

count of the improbability, if not impossibility of *Spirits.* So that it is plain the rejecting of the being and commerce of Dæmons or Infernal Spirits opens a door to the denial of the Deity, of which we can no otherwise conceive than that it is an *Eternal Spirit.*

There are *Other Doctrines* which advance Atheism, and may be reckon'd among the Dangerous Luxuriances of these Inquisitive Times. Such is the vilifying of the *Hebrew Text* of the Old Testament, the proclaiming it to be faulty and erroneous, in order to establishing the *Seventy's Version* as only Authentick. Such is the building the Authority of the Books of the Old Testament on the pretended inspiration of certain *Publick Scribes* or *Notaries* among the *Jews,* in imitation of such among the *Egyptians* ;
the

the avouching that the *Leaves* or *Volumes* on which thofe Books were wrote are mifplaced and put out of order; the profeffed declaring that the *Canonical Books* are not the *fame* that they were at firft, but that feveral words and paffages are left out. All mere Fiction and Conceit, unworthy of fo Excellent a Genius as *F. S*'s. Such alfo is the maintaining that the greateft part of the *Religious Rites* and *Conftitutions* which God himfelf fettled among the *Jews* were a Tranfcript of thofe that were in ufe among the *Idolatrous Pagan Nations*, and that the All-Wife Lawgiver borrow'd thofe immediately from thefe. The two former of thefe Attempts null the Authority of the Sacred Writings, and the laft of them difparages not only them but the Bleffed Founder of the Jewifh Oeco-

Oeconomy. I speak not this as if any of these Opinions can be thought to be True Reasons on which a man may ground his disesteem of the Scriptures, or of the Holy Doctrines contain'd in them, or of the Sacred Inditer of them; for they are the Sentiments but of a very few, and of those whose Learning, though it was exceeding great, had not wholly conquer'd their Prejudice, or freed them from Misapprehensions in some things. I cannot charge them with any direct design of favouring the Cause of Atheism, but ill-disposed men have made use of their Notions to that purpose. Wherefore, as we value the Reputation of our Religion, and the Honour of the Divine Author of it, let us be careful that we split not upon any of these *Rocks*, nor endanger our selves on any of the

Shallows

Shallows before mention'd, and thereby make Shipwrack of our Faith and Holy Profession, or so endanger our selves that we can hardly be brought off again.

I might in the last place take notice of a Plausible Conceit which hath been growing up to a considerable time, and now hath the fortune to come to some maturity. Not to speak of its reception, (if not its birth) among some *Foreign* Authors, chiefly *Socinians*, it seemed among our selves to be favour'd by that Learned, but Wavering, Prelate who writ the *Liberty of Prophesying*, and afterwards by another of his Order who compos'd * *The Naked Truth*. Lately it hath been revived by the Author of *the Naked Gospel:* and since more particularly fully and distinctly it hath been

---

* Chap. 1, Concerning the Articles of Faith.

maintain'd by the late Publisher of the *Reasonableness of Christianity, as deliver'd in the Scriptures.* He gives it us over and over again in these formal words, *viz.* that *nothing is required to be believed by any Christian man but this, that Jesus is the Messiah.* He contends that there is no other Article of Faith necessary to Salvation; this is a Full and Perfect Creed, and no person need concern himself in any other. This takes up about three quarters of his book, for he goes through the History of the *Evangelists* and the *Acts of the Apostles,* according to the order of Time (as he thinks) to give an account of this Proposition. But yet this Gentleman forgot, or rather wilfully omitted a plain and obvious passage in one of the Evangelists, *Go teach all nations, baptizing them in the name of the Father,* and of the *Son*, and of the Holy *Ghoſt*, *Mat.* 28. 19. From which it is plain, that all Proſelites to Chriſtianity, all that are adult Members of the Chriſtian Church, muſt be *taught*, as well as baptized, into the Faith of the *Holy Trinity*, Father, Son, and Holy Ghoſt. And if they muſt be *taught* this Doctrne (which is the peremptory Charge and Commiſſion here given to the Apoſtles, *Go teach*, &c.) then it is certain that they muſt *believe* it, for this Teaching is in order to Belief. This will be denied by none, I ſuppoſe, and conſequently more is required to be believed by Chriſtian men, and Members of Chriſt's Church, than that *Jeſus is the Meſſiah*. You ſee it is part of the *Evangelical Faith*, and ſuch as is neceſſary, abſolutely neceſſary, to make one a Member of the Chriſtian Church,

to

to believe a Trinity in Unity in the Godhead; or, in plainer terms, that though God is One as to his Essence and Nature, yet there are Three Persons in that Divine Essence, and that these Three Persons are really the One God: for we can't imagine that Men and Women should be required to be baptized into the Faith and Worship of any but the Only True God. This Epitomizer of the Evangelical Writings left out also that famous Testimony in *John* 1. 1. *In the beginning was the Word (*Christ Jesus*) and the Word was with God, and the Word was God.* Whence we are obliged to yield assent to this Article, that *Christ is the word of God.* And there is added in Verse 14. another indispensable Point of Faith, *viz.* that the *word was made Flesh,* i. e. that God was Incarnate, the same with 1 *Tim.* 3. 16.

3. 16. *God manifest in the Flesh.* And it follows in the same Verse of this first Chapter of St. *John*, that this *Word* is *the only begotten of the Father:* whence we are bound to believe the *Eternal*, though ineffable, *Generation of the Son of God.* Our Author likewise takes no notice that we are commanded *to believe the Father and the Son*, Joh. 14. 10, 11. and that *the Son is in the Father, and the Father in the Son*, which expresses their *Unity*. This is made an Article of Faith by our Saviour's particular and express Command. And other eminent parts of Christian Belief this Writer passes by, without having any regard to them, and yet pretends to present the World with a Compleat and Entire Account of all that is the matter of our Faith under the Gospel. This cannot but seem very

ry strange and unaccountable to any man of deliberate Thoughts, and who expects Sincerity from a Writer who makes some shew of it?

But this is not all; this Learned Gentleman, who with so much industry amasses together Quotations out of the *Gospels* and the *Acts of the Apostles*, yet is not pleas'd to proceed to the *Epistles*, and to give an Account of them as he did of the others; though the *Epistles* are as considerable a part of the *New Testament* as the *Gospels* and the *Acts*, and the Pen-men of them were equally inspired by the Holy Ghost. Can there be any Reason given of this partial dealing? Yes, it is most evident to any thinking and considerate person that he purposely omits the *Epistolary Writings* of the Apostles because they are fraught with

with *Other Fundamental Doctrines* besides that One which he mentions. There we are instructed concerning these Grand Heads of Christian Divinity, *viz.* the Corruption and Degeneracy of Humane Nature, with the True Original of it (the Defection of our First Parents) the Propagation of Sin and Mortality, our Restoration and Reconciliation by Christ's Blood, the Eminency and Excellency of his Priesthood, the Efficacy of his Death, the full Satisfaction thereby made to the Divine Justice, and his being made an All-sufficient Sacrifice for Sin. Here are peculiar Discoveries concerning Christ's Righteousness, and our Justification by it, concerning Election, Adoption, Sanctification, or the New Birth, and particularly Saving Faith, which is so signal

a part

the Causes of Atheism.

a part of it. Here the Nature of the Gospel, and the New Covenant, the Riches of God's Mercy in the way of Salvation by Jesus Christ, the Certainty of the Resurrection of Humane Bodies, and of the Future Glory, are fully displayed. These are the Matters of *Faith* contain'd in the *Epistles*, and they are essential and integral parts of the Gospel it self: and therefore it is no wonder that our Author, being sensible of this, would not vouchsafe to give us an Abstract of these Inspired Writings, but passes them by with some Contempt. And more especially (if I may conjecture) he doth this because he knew that there are so many and Frequent, and those so illustrious and eminent Attestations to the Doctrine of the ever to be Adored *Trinity* in these Epistles.

Nor is this any uncharitable conjecture, as the Reader may easily satisfie himself if he takes notice that this Writer interprets *the Son of God* to be no more than the *Messiah*; he expounds *John* 14. 9. &c. after the Antitrinitarian mode, whereas generally Divines understand some part of those words concerning the Divinity of our Saviour. He makes *Christ* and *Adam* to be *the Sons of God* in the same senses, *viz.* by their Birth, as the *Racovians* generally do, and so he interprets *Luke* 1. 35. *John* 5. 26. according to their Standard. When he proceeds to mention the *Advantages* and *Benefits* of Christ's Coming into the world, and appearing in the flesh, he hath not one syllable of his Satisfying for us, or by his Death purchasing Life and Salvation, or any thing that sounds like it.

the Causes of Atheism.

it. This and several other things which might be offered to the Reader, shew that he is all over Socinianiz'd; and moreover that his design was to exclude the belief of the Blessed *Trinity* in this Undertaking of his, *viz.* to prove that the believing of Christ to be the Messiah is the only Point of Faith that is necessary and saying. All the other Articles and Doctrines must fall a sacrifice to the Darling Notion of the Antitrinitarians, namely that Christ is not the True God, and coessential with his Father. For the sake of this one Point they are all dispatch'd out of the world, and are made by him Martyrs to this Cause. One could scarcely imagine that a person of Ingenuity and Good Sense should go this way to work. Which enclines me to think that the Ingenious

nious Gentleman who is suppos'd by some to be the Author of this Treatise is not really so. I am apt to believe that the world is impos'd upon in this matter, for in this present Attempt there are none of those Noble Strokes which are visible in that Person's Writings, and which have justly gain'd him a fair repute. That Vivacity of thought, that Elevation of mind, that Vein of Sense and Reason, yea and of Elocution too which runs through his Works are all extinct here: only he begins as 'twere to recover himself about the Close when he comes to speak of the Laws of Christian Morality. Some may attribute this Flatness to the Ill Cause he manages; but for my part, I question whether we have the right Author, I can't perswade my self but that there is an *Error*

of

of the Person: at least I will charitably presume so, because I have so good an opinion of the Gentleman who writ of *Humane Understanding* and *Education*.

But what is the ground of the foresaid Assertion? What makes him contend for One Single Article, with the Exclusion of all the rest? He pretends it is this, that all men ought to understand their Religion. And I agree with him in this; but I ask him, may not a man understand those Articles of Faith which I mention'd out of the *Gospel* and *Epistles*, if they be explain'd to him, as well as that One which he speaks of? Why then must there be but One Article, and no more? But he, notwithstanding this, goes on, and urges that there must be nothing in Christianity that is not plain, and exactly

actly level to all mens Mother-wit and common apprehension. For *God considered the poor of the world, and the bulk of mankind: the Christian Religion is suited to vulgar capacities,* and hath only * *such Articles as the labouring and illiterate man may comprehend.* *The Writers and Wranglers in Religion fill it with Niceties, and dress it up with Notions,* (viz. the Trinity, Christ's Satisfaction, &c.) *which they make necessary and fundamental parts of it.* But the bulk of mankind have not leisure for Learning and Logick: and therefore there must be no such doctrine as that concerning the *Trinity, the Incarnation of the Son of God,* and the like, which are above the capacity and comprehension of the Vulgar. And in the Entrance of his book he hath the same notion, for he tells us that

---

* P. 302. † P. 302.

the

the Scriptures are *a collection of writings designed by God for the instruction of the illiterate bulk of mankind,* (for he is much taken with this phrase, you see, *the bulk of mankind*) whereby he understands the Ignorant and Unlearned Multitude, the *Mob,* as he calls it in another place. Surely this Gentleman is afraid of *Captain Tom,* and is going to make a Religion for his Myrmidons: and to please them he gives them as little of this kind as he possibly can, he contracts all into One Article, and will trouble them with no more. Now then the sum of all that he aims at is this, that we must not have any Point of Doctrine whatsoever in our Religion that the *Mob* doth not at the very first naming of it perfectly understand and agree to. We are come to a fine pass indeed: the Venerable
Mob

Mob must be ask'd what we must *believe*: and nothing must be receiv'd as an Article of Faith but what those Illiterate Clubmen vote to be such. The *Rabble* are no *System-makers*, no *Creed-makers*; and therefore away with *Systems* and *Creeds*, and let us have but One Article, though it be with the defiance of all the rest, which are of equal necessity with that One.

Towards the close of his Enterprise he hath a fling (and that a Shrewd one) at the *Dissenters*, telling them that * *their Congregations and their Teachers understand not the Controversies at this time so warmly manag'd among them.* Nay the Teachers themselves have been pleas'd to make him their Confessor, and to acknowledge to him that

---
* Page. 303.

the Causes of Atheism. 119

they understand not the difference in debate between them. Why? becaufe they (as well as the Conformifts) have Obfcure Notions and Speculations, fuch as *Juftification*, the *Trinity*, *Satisfaction*, &c. terms that all the *bulk of mankind* are unacquainted with: whereas Religion fhould have no Difficulties and Myfteries in it. The very Manner of every thing in Chriftianity muft be clear and intelligible, every thing muft be prefently comprehended by the weakeft noddle, or elfe it is no part of *Religion*, efpecially of *Chriftianity*, which yet is call'd the * *Myftery of Godlinefs*: but this being in the *Epiftles*, it is no great matter; we are not to mind what they fay.

Thus we fee what is the Reafon why he reduces all Belief to

---
* 1 Tim. 3. 16.

that one Article before rehearsed: as if the other Main Points which I produced were not as *easily learnt* and *understood* as This; as if there were any thing more difficult in this Proposition [The Father, Son and Holy Ghost are One God, or Divine Nature] than in that other [Jesus is the Messiah]. Truly if there be any Difficulty, it is in this latter, for here is an *Hebrew* word first to be explain'd before the *Mob* (as he stiles it) can understand the Proposition. Why therefore doth this Author, who thinks it absurd * *to talk Arabick* to the Vulgar, talk *Hebrew* to them, unless he be of opinion (which no body else is of) that they understand this Language better than that? Or, suppose he tells the Rabble that *Messiah* signi-

---

* Page 302.

the Caufes of Atheifm. 121

fies *Anointed*, what then ? Unlefs he explains that word to them, it is ftill unintelligible. So that it appears hence that this Article which he hath fpent fo much time about, is no more level to the underftanding of the Vulgar then that of the *Holy Trinity*, yea it is not fo much.

To conclude, this Gentleman and his fellows are refolved to be *Unitarians*; they are for *One* Article of Faith, as well as *One* Perfon in the Godhead; and there is as much reafon for one as the other, that is, none at all. But it doth not become me perhaps to pronounce this fo peremptorily, and therefore I appeal to the Judicious and Impartial Reader; defiring him to judge of what I have fuggefted. But this I will fay, if thefe Learned men were not highly prejudiced and prepossessed, they would discern the Evil and Mischief of their Assertion: they would perceive that when the Catholick Faith is thus brought down to One Single Article, it will soon be reduced to none: the Unit will dwindle into a Cypher.

The Proper Remedy here is to consider that it is unlawful * *to add unto, or diminish ought from* the Written Word: yea, a *Curse* is threatned against those that † *add to or take away* from the Scriptures; for if it be criminal, and deserves a Curse to deal thus with the book of *Deuteronomy* or of the *Revelation*, then by the same reason those that *add to* or *detract* from any *other* part of the Holy Scriptures are undeniably guilty, and are obnoxious to the Divine Plagues. I

---

* Deut. 4. 2. † Rev. 22. 18, 19.

hope

the Causes of Atheism.

hope such as practise the *latter* will seriously think of it, and for the future believe themselves concern'd to embrace *All* the necessary and fundamental Articles of Faith, as well as *One* of them.

Thus I have briefly discover'd the Springs and Sources of *Atheism*, and I have endeavour'd all along (more or less) to stop them up, and hinder the current of them. Now, for the close of all, let me add these *Inferences* from the whole,

I. We ought to bewail the spreading Atheism of this Age wherein we live. Of old there were but few that openly profess'd it. There are reckon'd up *four* several sorts or forms of Atheism by a late * Learned Writer, viz. *Anaximandrian, Democritick, Stoical, Stratonical*, and yet

---
* Dr. *Cudworth*'s Intellectual System.

there was scarcely one of these that was a downright denying of a God. Some have given *Diagoras*, *Theodorus*, *Protagoras*, the title of *Atheists*, and have thought them to be absolutely such: but others, upon a strict search, are of opinion, that they deserv'd not that infamous Name; yea, they find that they were great Asserters of a Deity. The first of these was accused of Atheism, and banish'd for it by the *Athenians*; not that he denied a God, but because he derided the Feigned Gods of his time, whom the *Athenians* had such a reverence for. The second passes for an Atheist; but those who have narrowly enquired into things tell us, that he got that Name because he spoke against the Idolatrous Worship of the *Grecians*, and had a kindness (it is probable) for another Religion: for

being

being a *Cyrenian*, and acquainted with King *Ptolomee*, he came to have some Intercourse with the *Jews of Alexandria*, and had some notice of the True God. The third was reputed and call'd by some an Atheist because he doubted of the Truth and Reality of the *Gentile Gods*. So *Anaxagoras* (another Greek Philosopher) was arraign'd for Atheism by the *Athenians* because he denied the Sun to be God, and freely discours'd against the other Pagan Deities. Thus the malicious Accusers of *Socrates* represented him as an Enemy to the Gods: part of the Crime charged on him, and for which he was condemn'd, was his speaking against the Traditions and Fables of the *Poets* concerning the Gods, and his declaring them to be lewd and wicked. To give this Great Man his

his due, he was so far from being an Atheist, that he died a Martyr for a Deity. Only to gratifie the Vulgar, and that he might not go off unlamented, after he had drank his Poison he requested his Friends to offer a Cock for him to *Æsculapius*. Some put *Democritus* into the Catalogue of the Ancient Atheists, but if we read his Life in *Laertius*, we shall find that they have little reason to do so. *Lucretius* is the most suspicious man of all, and *Lucian* may be join'd with him, the former a serious, the latter a jocular Atheist.

But it is sad to consider that the number of this sort of men hath been exceedingly augmented since. * *David Perron* undertook in the presence of King *Henry* the Third of *France*, to prove that there is

---
* *L'Histoire d' Henr.* 3

the Causes of Atheism.

no God. *Merſennus*, in his Commentary on *Geneſis*, tells us, that in the Year when he wrote it, *viz.* 1623. there was a vaſt multitude of them in *France:* there were at leaſt fifty thouſand Atheiſts in the City of *Paris* at that time, and in one houſe ſometimes a dozen were to be found. A worthy * Author, whom I had occaſion to mention before, acquaints us on his own Knowledge, that Atheiſm was very common and rampant in moſt parts of *Italy*. Not to mention *Machiavel*, *Aretine*, &c. it cannot be denied that *Vanenus* openly declared and profeſs'd himſelf an Atheiſt, and died ſo at the Stake. Indeed I am apt to ſuſpect thoſe who tell us there are ſcarcely any of this Perſwaſion in the World. Thus † one declares that *he hath*

---

* In his *Europæ Speculum*. † An Eſſay in a Letter from *Oxford*.

travelled many *Countries*, yet could never meet with any *Atheists*, which are few if any: all the noise and clamour is against *Castles in the Air*, i. e. such and no other he fancies them to be. But to come nearer, our Own Nation hath produced too many of this kind. Even in this Civilized Christian Protestant Country there are those that are infected with this Cursed Infidelity, and defie all Religion and a God. It is an unquestionable Truth, that there are in this great City of the Kingdom constant *Cabals* and *Assemblies* of Profess'd Atheists, where they debate the Great Point of the Existence of an Infinite Spirit that governs the World, and in the close determine in the Negative. I have sometime accidentally happen'd into the Company of, and held Discourse with some that acknowledge they belong to that Society; and they

they have not been aſhamed to own whatever is done in it. Mr. *Hobbes* is their Great Maſter and Lawgiver. I find that they pay a huge reverence to him. If they acknowledge any *Divine Thing,* it is *He.* If they own any *Scriptures,* they are his *Writings.* The Language that I lately met with from the mouth of one that was, I ſuppoſe, a *Wellwiſher* (according to his poor ability) to Mr. *Hobbes*'s *Mathematicks,* was this, *His Leviathan is the beſt Book in the world next to the Bible: He himſelf was a Man of great Piety, and is ſpoken againſt by none but the Prieſts.* And whom do they (for this man ſpeaks the ſenſe of the reſt) mean by *Prieſts* but the *Miniſters of Religion?* So they would have a *Bible* and *Piety* without theſe; which is as much as to ſay, they would have neither of them. But indeed this man had a way of being ſomething

thing more plausible than his Fellows, and would vouchsafe to mention the *Bible* and *Piety*, and thereby seem as it were to allow of such things; whereas Others are wont to laugh at *them* as well as at the Persons they call *Priests*, for they go together. I may say truly, it is grown *Fashionable* to deride whatever is Sacred, and to talk like an *Atheist*. In some Companies it shall be question'd whether a Person be a *Gentleman* if he does not give Proofs of his being Prophane. To defend the wildest Principles, and to ridicule Religion, is counted one certain mark of a *Wit*. He that doth not shew his Raillery against Virtue and Goodness, and speaks not contemptibly of God and Religion, is not *a Man of Parts*. This is the Sentiment and Perswasion of a great part of this Nation. I would not libel the Land of our Nativity; yea,

yea, I rather heartily wish that what I have said on this occasion might receive a Confutation. But it is too evident that I speak truth; it is too manifest to be denied that there are every where considerable numbers of men who openly renounce the Existence of God. *David*'s Atheist was modest, and only *said in his Heart, There is no God*; on which account some Atheistical Spirits now-a-days may think perhaps he deserved the Title of *Fool* which the Psalmist gives him. But these count themselves a *Wiser* rank of Atheists, because they *say this with their mouths*, and speak it aloud, audibly proclaiming their Opinion, and being very zealous to gain Proselytes to it.

2. Let us abhor the Converse and Society of those Persons whom we know to be of this Character. And truly they are very common every where.

where. It is prodigious to see how they daily encrease. There is scarcely a Town where there are not some that may justly be reckon'd in this number. Do not mistake me. There are some deluded People who are apt to censure all as *Atheists* that are not of their way. The * Primitive Christians were thus stigmatized, and usually called by that name because they did not comply with the Pagan Worship and Usages. If a man discourses not according to some mens fond Notions and Bigotisms; if he speaks against their superstitious Practices, he presently hath this Brand set upon him. There are those that call all Persons *Atheists* and *Hypocrites* that hold not the same Principles with themselves. Yea, if a man be a great Student in Philosophy, some weaker People may be apt to fix this Character on

---

* Just. Mart. Apol. 2.

him.

him. As heretofore all that had skill in *Mathematicks* were said and thought to deal in Art Magick; so in the opinion of some at this day men of great Art and Learning are voted *Atheists* by them, and almost every *Physician* hath this Censure past on him by men of weak minds. But I hope none of those I now speak to are so unwise and weak, or at least not so uncharitable and censorious as to bestow this Ignominious Epithet on those to whom it doth not belong. By an *Atheist* or a person very much disposed to be so, I mean one that hath an Enmity to the very notion of a Divine Infinite Being, a Supreme Immaterial Substance, that is the Soveraign Author of Nature, and the First Cause of all things, from whom all things were, and on whom they depend. I mean such a one as owns no Allegiance to this Divine Ruler and

and Soveraign, and in his Words and Actions difcovers this to the World. And accordingly he is one that acknowledges not the Infinite Power, Wifdom, Goodnefs, and Juftice of God in the Government of all things: he fpeaks irreverently of all that appertains to Religion and Godlinefs: he laughs at the profound Myfteries and fublime Doctrines of Chriftianity: he endeavours always to diminifh the efteem of Sacred things: yea, he will be jefting and drolling on them if he hath any Talent that way. If he be open-hearted, and not upon the Referve, he will tell them that Religion is a mere Invention of Politick Heads to awe the Multitude, and to keep the World in good order. He is one that blafts Religion with the ignominious Title of a Popular Cheat, and labours to perfwade others to do the like. Where

do

you find these Characters in any person, you may conclude without breach of Charity, that he is an *Atheist.*

And it is the Company of such that I exhort you to beware of, and wholly to avoid. It is almost incredible that such great numbers should be every day led away with this *Ignis Fatuus*, and plung'd into Bogs and Mire, never to be pluck'd out thence. Therefore take heed what Society you mingle your selves with in this Dangerous Age. Sit not with the known Despisers of God and Religion, for they will insensibly instill their poison into you. By frequent associating with them you will learn to resemble them. Wherefore fly from them as from a Serpent, and be not prevail'd with by any Entreaties or Threats to hold Correspondence with them. Assure your selves of this, that the Title of

Atheist is the most Reproachful and Detestable one imaginable, though some of late who glory in their shame entertain other thoughts. Nay, some of these Persons seem to be partly sensible of it, and change the name into that of *Deist*. At this day *Atheism* it self is slily call'd *Deism* by those that indeed are *Atheists*. Though they retain the thing, yet they would disguise it by a false Name, and thereby hide the Heinousness of it. But let us not be deceived and blinded by pretended Shews, but throughly apprehend the Vileness of this Opinion which some endeavour to palliate. It is a very denying the Creed of Nature, it is a Renuntiation of that which the very Devils believe, and tremble at. It is briefly but fully represented in St. *Cyprian*'s words, * *This*

---

* *Hæc est summa delicti nolle agnoscere quem ignorare non possis.* De Vanit. Idol.

(saith

(faith he) *is the sum of this most heinous Crime, that those who are guilty of it wilfully refuse to acknowledge Him whom they cannot be ignorant of.* For their own Beings and Natures furnish them with Arguments for a God: and if they did not obstinately shut their eyes, they must needs behold a Deity. Therefore to be *Atheists*, or *without God in the world* (as the * Apostle speaks) cannot but be a Great Prodigy; it is Unaccountable almost (if the Degeneracy of Mankind were not so great as it is) that the *World* it self should not administer to mens Thoughts Convictive Arguments of a Divinity. Whence it hath been obferv'd by a very Wife Man, that there never was any Miracle wrought by God to convert an *Atheist*, because the Light of Nature might have led him to confess

---
* Ephes. 2. 12.

a God. This shews how detestable and pernicious *Atheism* is; and much more might be said to this purpose. Wherefore I hope I need not multiply words when I call upon you to keep out of the Company of those men who you know are infected with this hellish Poison.

3. Let us labour to work in our selves and others a profound Sense of that *Great God* with whom we have to do. Generally the Belief of a Deity is from Custom and Education, because it is the Perswasion of the Place and the Persons we converse with: but we should not content our selves with this, but arrive to the Knowledge of the true *Grounds* and *Reasons* of this Belief. Seeing this is the First thing in Religion, and no Man can be Religious and Vertuous unless he believes there is a God, let us fortifie our Minds against Atheism by those
seve-

several *Arguments* and *Considerations* which are wont to be propounded by Learned and Religious * Writers: that we may as throughly be perswaded of this Great Truth as of our own Being, which a Great Philosopher makes one of his First and Indubitable Principles.

But especially view the Works of the Creation, and perswade your selves of this, that a Material World without an Immaterial Cause of it, is mere Nonsense. Look abroad, and behold the Heavens and the Earth, and all the Furniture of them; there you may believe a Deity, because you do as 'twere see it. The Creator is made visible by his Works. Every thing in the Sensible World is an † Image, a Picture, a

---

* *Fab. Faventini Disp. 4. adv. Atheos. Tho. Campanella Spizel Scrutin. Atheismi. Muller. Atheismus devictus. Jan. & Joach. Jan. Disputat. contr. Atheos.* Dr. *More*, Mr. *Smith*, Sir *Charles Wolsley*, Dr. *Tenison*, (now Archbishop of *Cant.*) Dr. *Cudworth*, Dr. *Barrow*.

† Εἰκὼν, εἴδωλον, ἴχνος. Plato.

Foot-

Footstep of the Deity. From this Exquisite Fabrick we infallibly gather the Existence of its All-wise Architect and Moderator. Of which I shall give the Reader a particular Demonstration in a short time. And that you may effectually extirpate Atheism out of your minds, frequently peruse the H. Scriptures. Read God in his own Book. There you will certainly inform your selves concerning the Superintendence of Spiritual or Immaterial Agents, *viz.* *Angels*, which makes way for the Belief of a *God*, who is a Spirit. There you will meet with those Wonderful Operations and Events which can no ways be solv'd without granting an Omnipotent and All-wise Disposer of things. And there you will find this Supreme Governour of the World communicating his Will and Pleasure to Mankind. I question not but one great

great Reason (and I might have mention'd it among the rest) why men are so disposed to be *Atheists*, is because they never, or very seldom, consult this Holy Volume: they refuse to hear God Himself speaking to them in these Writings. Wherefore I recommend to you the serious and frequent reading of the Bible as the most effectual means to confirm you in the Belief of a Deity. Assure your selves that this Book is the best Antidote against Atheism.

4. and lastly, Labour to be truly Religious and Holy; beg the Divine Assistance to sanctifie you in your Hearts and Lives; and thereby you will be let into the intimate knowledge of this Grand Verity which I have been discoursing of. You will then more sensibly understand and be convinced of it than by all the Arguments that
can

can be offer'd: or rather, this one will make all the rest effectual. Whereas on the contrary, Men of Unsanctified Minds and Profane Lives despise and scoff at that of which they have no experience, and will not believe the Existence and Power of God which they never felt. Strive then by an Inward Experiment to confute Atheism: so that you may not have any Inclination to *say in your hearts* (though you do not utter it with your tongues) *There is no God*, but that you may be so strongly convinced of the contrary Truth that you may be able to assert it with a firm and unshaken Belief, and from an internal sense of it on your hearts, to attest the reality of it to the whole World.

FINIS.

ERRAT.
Pag. 104. lin. 8. dele *to*.

Socinianism Unmask'd.

A
DISCOURSE
Shewing the
Unreasonableness
Of a Late
Writer's OPINION

Concerning the Necessity of only
One Article of Christian Faith;

And of his other Assertions in his late Book,
Entituled,

The Reasonableness of Christianity as deliver'd in the Scriptures, and in his *Vindication* of it.

With a Brief Reply to another (professed) Socinian Writer.

By *JOHN EDWARDS*, B. D. and sometime Fellow of S. *John*'s College in *Cambridge*.

LONDON: Printed for *J. Robinson* at the *Golden Lyon*, and *J. Wyat* at the *Rose* in S. *Paul*'s Church-yard. M DC XC VI.

THE
INTRODUCTION.

THE following Discourse (which was finish'd above two months ago, but by reason of some Intervening Occurrences found not its way to the Press) is design'd against the undertaking of a late Author in his book which bears the Title of *the Reasonableness of Christianity*, &c. But the Writer himself is wonderfully pleased with his Lying hid, and being No Body. I grant there may be Reasons why a man may sometimes conceal his Name, and not prefix it to the Book he is Au-

The Introduction.

thor of. But there are some Reasons that are proper and peculiar to this Writer's circumstances, for this is perfectly after the Mode of our late *English Racovian* Writers, who constantly appear *Nameless*, and accordingly herein he shews himself to be of the right *Racovian* breed. And another good reason is this (which indeed argues something of Modesty) he would not set a *Christian Name* before that book wherein he so grosly abuses *Christianity*, and renounces the greatest part of it.

I will not wast time, and trouble the Reader and my self about guessing who this Writer is. Out of Christian good will and charity I am backward to believe that he who is vogued to be the Father of these Extravagant Conceits, is really so. I will still perswade my self

The Introduction.

self that there is *an Error of the Person*; upon which account I shall be more free than otherwise I should have been.

But to come to the Book it self; there was (to express it in the most Learned and Rhetorical Stile of our Author himself) a *great flutter, noise and buz,* raised about it, even while it was yet under the Printers hands. There were certain Factors and Emissaries who extravagantly extolled it, and it was observ'd this Applause came from the *Racovian* quarter. Those of that way knew before it came out that it was in favour of their Cause: whence it was that they so mightily raised the Expectations of those they convers'd with, and highly magnified this Piece before the world had seen it. And as soon as it was blessed with the sight of it, their language ran to an exorbitant heighth: as if *Christianity* had been never known before the time of the compiling of this book. All that went before this Author were deluded Creatures, and were perfect Strangers to the Articles of the Christian Faith, and to Christianity it self. Now is risen up an Infallible Teacher: all must obsequiously repair to this Great Oracle. Now the *Socinians* have another Champion, now they look brisk upon it, and the day is their own. Now Converts come in apace, and the Youth begin to have a *Polonian* Aspect: and in a short time we shall have a Brood of *Socinians*, we shall be stock'd with Young *Racovians*.

And to let you into the whole Project, this is the short account of it, *Socinianism* was to be erected

at

The Introduction.

at this time (they can stay no longer) and in order to that all hands are to be employed, *i. e.* all that they can get. Among others they thought and made choice of a Gentleman, who they knew would be extraordinarily useful to them; and he it is probable was as forward to be made use of by them, and presently accepted of the Office which was assigned him. Now, thinks he, I had best to make use of this opportunity, and to set up for a *Divine*. Not only *the Illiterate bulk of mankind, but their Reverences and Right Reverences* (to use the words of *a * Writer of our own Brotherhood*) shall come to Me to have their understandings inform'd

---

* The Exceptions of Mr. *E.* against the *Reasonableness of Christianity*, &c. examined.

The Introduction.

form'd, for we have but a sorry unthinking sort of *Teachers* now a-days, whether they be Conformists or otherwise: I could never approve of their *Syſtematick* genius, their doating upon *Creeds* and *Confeſſions*, and rendring our Faith cumberſom and burdenſom. It may be even theſe men will give ear to what a *Thoughtful Muſing* Man dictates to them, though they never *think* themſelves, but take all upon truſt, and ſwallow *Epiſtles* and *Goſpel* together. I have attained to ſuch a heighth and perfection of knowledg that I am able to inſtruct theſe people after another rate. I muſt tell them (which I know they will look very ſtrangely upon) that the Apoſtles, when they wrote the *Epiſtles* to their Chriſtian Converts, deſigned not to trouble their heads

with

with any *Articles* or *Truths* that were neceſſarily to be believed, they only dropt a few *Occaſional* Documents. And it may be now and then that *One Article* which I have propounded to the world may be hook'd in by the by: but that is no place to look for any Neceſſary and Fundamental Truth of Chriſtianity, which is abſolutely to be believ'd by us.

This ſeems to be Novel Doctrine, and ſo indeed it is, for I have the honour to be the firſt famous Inventer of it; but I doubt not but in a ſhort time I ſhall not only propagate this, but the *Cauſe* to which it is ſubſervient, in a wonderful manner. To this purpoſe I will carry it cunningly: whileſt the *Double-Column'd Prints* are openly and in a down-right way advancing the Cauſe, I will do as much
ſer-

service under-hand. They look directly towards *Poland* or *Transylvania*, they publickly profess themselves to be *Socinus*'s Followers, but I'll be upon the Reserve, and so disguise my self that it shall be very difficult to discover me. I will make the world believe that I never heard of such a man as *Socinus*: and if they tell me that I speak his very language as perfectly as if I were a Native of *Sienna*, I'll face them down that I had it not by fingring of any Socinian Authors, but by a kind of *Natural Revelation*.

Well, this cause must be carried on, and I can do it as well as any man by maintaining that there is but *One Article of Christian Faith necessarily to be believ'd to make a man a Christian*, necessarily to be believ'd in order to salvation. For if there be

The Introduction.

be but One Point neceſſary to be believ'd, then the doctrines concerning the *Trinity*, concerning the *Incarnation* and *Divinity of Chriſt*, concerning his *Satisfaction*, &c. are rendred unneceſſary as to the making us Chriſtians. And this I will ſhove on under the colour of being ſerviceable to *the bulk of Mankind*, of being obliging and merciful to the *Multitude* and *Rabble*, and *Poor People*; though (to ſay the Truth) I ſhew my ſelf to be ſo far from obliging the Multitude that I do them an infinite deal of Miſchief. Yet if I compaſs my End, it is enough, and I care for no more. And my End is this, to hale in *Socinianiſm* after a new manner.

You ſee what the *Muſing* of this Gentleman comes to: and I was ſo unhappy a man as to find it out,

to

to take notice of it, and to discover it to the world in a late *Discourse* which I publish'd: and thereby I have extremely exasperated this New Undertaker and his Adherents. I do not wonder at it, for now their Intrigues are laid open, their *Racovian* Plot is detected, and all their Measures are thereby broken.

But to keep up their hearts, a*Vindication*(as it is call'd)of thisTreachery is publish'd by him who was appointed to be the Chief Tool in this work. Here he makes it his business to defend his New Paradox, and to shore his Notion up again with some crazy props. Throughout the whole he is pleas'd to Criticize with some Magisterialness and Pertness on the Reflections which I made on his book

The Introduction.

book. And now it is my turn again to be Critick, and I shall discharge the Task with all impartiality and integrity. It is true, there is nothing of any Moment, nothing Weighty and Argumentative in what he hath offered, and therefore some in whose Judgment I could confide, would have prevailed with me to add no more on this Subject, which they were perswaded I had before sufficiently cleared: but partly to shew somewhat further the great Danger and Mischief of this Writer's Opinion, partly to prevent the Seduction of some well-meaning persons who may be apt to be led away by his smooth Pretences, (for though his Cavils and Evasions be weak, yet they may chance to light into the Hands of some Weak

Rea-

The Introduction.

Readers, such as are not well establish'd in their notions : Wherefore not on the account of his Petty Objections, but for the sake of these persons I reassume this Argument) and partly to lay open the Wilful Mistakes and Gross Dissimulation (as I take it) of this Writer, and partly to gratifie those Gentlemens expectations who with some impatience seem to long for a Reply, I have once again undertaken to employ the Press upon this occasion. But the Chief and Principal Design, as well as Motive, of my appearing again in this Cause is to assert and defend the *Christian Faith* which this Author hath misrepresented, maim'd and abused. To which purpose I will set before the Reader the Heads of his pretended *Vindication*, and in the face of

The Introduction.

of the world make it appear how falſly and perfidiouſly he hath acted in the Cauſe of Religion. And may it be the Readers Prayer (as well as it is mine) that this Enterprize may tend to the Glory and Honour of *God the Father*, *God the Son*, and *God the Holy Ghoſt* (Three Glorious Perſons in One ever to be Adored Deity) and to the Edification of the *Chriſtian* Church. *Amen.*

Jan. 27.
169⅚.

ERRATA.

PAge 17. line. 1. read *World.* p. 22. l. 18. for *Chrift.* r. *Jefus.* p. 54. l. 20. r. *Sylburgius.* p. 85. l. 9. r. *Racovians.* p. 87. l. 23 after *Jefus* insert *Chrift.* p. 116. line 3. after *done* make the other part of the *Parenthesis.* p. 117. l. 18. after *if* insert *the truth were known, I believe it would appear that.* p. 120. l. 17. r. *telling.* p. 125. l. 8. r. *him.* p. 128. l. 21. after *hath* insert *bad.* p. 131. l. 13. after *religion* insert *who is so near a-kin to one that is voted a Socinian in the Brief Hiftory of the Unitarians.* p. 135. l. 11. r. *Socinianiz'd.*

A Late WRITER's
Unreasonable Opinions
CONFUTED.

CHAP. I.

The first General Charge against the Late Writer, viz. That he unwarrantably crowds all the Necessary Articles of Faith into One, *with a design of favouring* Socinianism. *He endeavours to shift off the Enditement, but is cast by his own words. His wilful mistake about the Article of the* Deity. *He labours in vain to split One Article into Two. It is shew'd that besides the bare believing of* Jesus to be the Messias, *it is necessary to know and believe the Fall of* Adam, *whereby Sin and Death entred into the World, and were derived to his posterity. It is necessary to know and believe* Who the Messias is; *whether he be God or Man, or both: on*

B *which*

which will follow the *neceſſary belief of the Holy* Trinity. *It is requiſite to have a right conception concerning our* Recovery *and* Reſtauration *by the* Meſſias, *i. e. to know what he undertook and did for us, and to be acquainted with the Great* Privileges *beſtow'd upon us by him. It is of neceſſity to believe what the* Meſſias *requires of Us. It is undoubted matter of our belief, that our Salvation ſprings from the mere Favour and Grace of God through* Chriſt Jeſus, *and not from any works or merits of ours. It is indiſpenſably requiſite, that we believe the Doctrin of the* Reſurrection, *of the* Final Judgment, *and of* Eternal Life.

I Will now betake my ſelf to the Task which is before me, after I have told the Reader, that I intend not to imitate our Nameleſs Author in his Childiſh Flouriſhes, in his Spruce and Starched Sentences, and in his Impotent Jeſtings, which are ſprinkled up and down his *Vindication.* Nor will I follow him in his Impertinencies and Incoherencies, in his trifling Excurſions to eke out his two ſheets and a half. I will not reſemble him in his

little

Opinions Confuted.

Little Artifices of evading, in his weak and feeble Struglings with a Strong Truth. I will not perfonate him in the Confufion and Diforder of his Reply, for it feems he had forgot, that it is one fign of a *Well-bred, a Well taught Man*, * *to anfwer to the firft in the firft place*, and fo in order. I will not imitate him in his Dry Common Places, in his Set of Words and Phrafes, of Sayings and Apothegms, which would have ferv'd on any other occafion, as the Intelligent Reader cannot but take notice. Much lefs will I comply with him in his Angry fits and Paffionate Ferments, which, tho he ftrives to palliate, are eafily difcernible, for he feels himfelf Wounded, and is not able to difguife it. I will betake my felf, I fay, to the prefent Concern with great application and mindfulnefs, fully making good my *Former Charges* againft his Book, and clearing my own from thofe forry Objections and Cavils which he hath fince rais'd againft it. In the whole management I will fincerely acquaint the Reader firft with *his own words*, and then offer my Refutation of them: and all along I will be

---

* *Mifhn. Tract. Avoth* c. 5

be careful to banish all Indecent Reflections; unless those shall be counted such which are purely grounded on his own expressions, and which his Freedom of Language necessarily and unavoidably administers to me.

The Main *Charges* are these. 1. That he unwarrantably crowded all the Necessary Articles of Faith into *One*, with a design of favouring *Socinianism*. 2. That he shew'd his good will to this Cause by interpreting those Texts which respect the *Holy Trinity*, after the Antitrinitarian mode. 3. That he gave proof of his being *Socinianiz'd* by his utter silence about *Christ's satisfying for us*, and purchasing Salvation by vertue of his Death, when he designedly undertook to enumerate the *Advantages* and *Benefits* which accrue to mankind by Christ's coming into the World. And in the making good of these Particular Charges, I shall (as I did before) evidence to the World that this Writer hath not only a design to cherish *Socinianism*, but at the same time to make way for *Atheism*.

I begin with the First, on which I will enlarge more than on any of the rest; because it comprehends in it several

Opinions Confuted.

veral other Particulars, and becaufe in difcuffing of this, I fhall have opportunity to lay open the Sophiftry and Diffimulation of this *Vindicator*, and likewife to difcover to the Reader how Mifchievous and Pernicious his Defign is. Firft, it is obfervable that this Guilty Man would be fhifting off the Enditement by excepting againft the *formality of the Words*, as if fuch were not to be found in his Book. But when doth he do this? In the clofe of it, when his matter was exhaufted, and he had nothing elfe to fay, *Vindic.* p. 38. Then he bethinks himfelf of this Salvo, whereas he had generally before pleaded to the formal Enditement, and had thereby owned it to be True. And indeed he can do no other, for it was the main work he fet himfelf about to find but *One Article* of Faith in all the Chapters of the four *Gofpels* and the *Acts of the Apoftles*: and accordingly he over and over again declares, that there is but that One Truth (viz. *Jefus is the Meffiah*) *neceffarily to be affented to by Chriftians*, or (as he fometimes words it) *abfolutely required to make a man a Chriftian, or a member of Chrift*. This is the *SOLE Doctrin prefs'd and requir'd to be believ'd*
in

in the whole tenour of our Saviour's and his Apostles preaching. p. 192. of his *Reasonableness of Christianity*. And again in the same place. *This was the ONLY Gospel Article of Faith which was Preached to them.* This he often inculcates, having left out several confiderable passages in the very *Gospels,* and having thrown aside the *Epistles,* as if they were no part of the New Testament, hoping that some of his Readers would be bubbled by this means.

And when I told him of his *One Article*, he knew well enough that I did not exclude the Article of the *Deity,* for that is a Principle of *Natural Religion*; whereas, I only took notice of his passing by and wholly omitting those points which are *Evangelical.* Yet he willfully mistakes me in this, p. 27. of his *Vindication*, and faith he doth not deny the necessary belief of a *Deity*, or *One only True God*; and so the belief of the *Messias* with that makes Two Articles. Thus he would persuade the Reader, that I misunderstood him, and that I tax'd him with setting up One Article, when he acknowledges two. But the Reader sees his Shuffling; for my Discourse did not treat (neither doth his Book

Opinions Confuted. 7

Book run that way) of Principles of *Natural Religion*, but of the *Revealed one*, and Particularly the *Chriſtian*. Accordingly this was it which I taxed him with, that of all the Principles and Articles of Chriſtianity he choſe out but *One* as neceſſarily to be believed to make a Man a Chriſtian.

And though ſince he hath tried to ſplit this One into two, p. 28. yet he labours in vain, for *to believe Jeſus to be the Meſſias* amounts to the ſame, with *believing him to be a King or Ruler*, his being *Anointed* (*i. e.* being the *Meſſias*) including that in it. Yet he hath the Vanity to add in great Characters, THESE ARE ARTICLES, as if the putting them into theſe *Great Letters* would make one Article two. Such is the fond fancy and conceitedneſs of the Gentleman, whereas in other places he hath formally declared, that there is but *One Article* that is the neceſſary Matter of Faith. This I had juſt reaſon to except againſt; and now I will give a farther account of my doing ſo, by ſhewing that, beſides that One Fundamental Principle or Article which he ſo often mentions, there are *Others* that are as neceſſarily to be believed to make a

B 4 Man

Man a *Christian*, yea to give him the denomination of a *Believer*, in the sense of the Gospel. Several of these I particularly, but barely enumerated in my former *Discourse*, and now I will distinctly insist on the most of them, and let the Reader see, that it is as necessary for a Convert to Christianity to give assent to *them*, as to that other he so frequently specifies.

This Proposition, that *by one man sin entred into the World, and death by sin:* and this which follows, *Death passed upon all men, for as much as all men have sinned*, Rom. 5. 12. and that other, that even *the Regenerate* (for the Apostle speaks of himself and the Converted Ephesians) *are by nature the Children of wrath, as well as others*, Eph. 2. 3. these, I say, are as absolutely necessary to be known, assented to, and believed, in order to our being *Christians* as this Proposition, *Jesus is the Messias, or Sent of God.* For I ask, what was the end of his being sent? Was it not to Help Mankind, to rescue and deliver them from some Evil? And where can we be inform'd concerning the Rise and Nature of this Evil, but in the Sacred and Inspired Writings? And do not these foresaid Texts, which we find in St. *Paul's Epistles*, acquaint us with the true Source and Quality of our condition by nature? Do they not discover the Root of Mans Misery, *viz.* the Apostacy of *Adam* (for he is that *one Man*) and the dreadful Consequences of it, expressed by *Death* and *Wrath*? And is this set down to no purpose in these Inspired *Epistles*? Is it not requisite that we should know it and believe it? Yea, is not this absolutely requisite? For it is impossible any one should firmly imbrace, or so much as seriously attend to the Doctrin of the *Messias*, unless he be persuaded that *He stands in need of him*. And can he be persuaded of this unless he be acquainted with his Degenerate and Miserable State, his universal Depravity and innate Proness to what is Vitious, and with the true Original of it? *viz.* The voluntary Defection and Fall of our First Parents, and with that the loss of our Happiness. The word *Messias* is an insignificant term till we have a belief of this: Why then is there a Treatise published to tell the World, that the bare belief of a *Messias* is all that is required of a Christian?

Again,

Again, it is not only necessary to know that *Jesus is the Messias*, but also to know and believe *who* this *Jesus*, this *Messias* is, *viz.* whether he be *God* or *Man*, or both. For every one will grant that there is a Vast Difference between the one and the other, as much as there is betwixt Infinite and Finite; and therefore that we may have a due apprehension concerning the *Messias*, it is absolutely necessary, that we should believe him to be what he is declared to be in the Infallible Writings, *viz. God* as well as *Man*. *The Word was God,* John 1. 1. *The Word was made Flesh,* v. 14. And this *Word* is *the Only begotten of the Father*, in the same Verse. *God was manifest in the Flesh*, 1 Tim. 3. 16. He is called not only *God* in these places, and in several others, but he is stil'd *the True God*, 1 John 5. 20. and *the Great God*, Tit. 2. 13. *The Lord of all*, Acts 10. 36. *God blessed for ever,* Rom. 9. 5. Hence we must conclude, that there is a necessity of believing the *Messias* to be *the very God*, of the same Essence with the Father and the Holy Ghost, for these are the two other *Persons* included in the Deity. So that hence it will follow, that it is requisite to believe the Holy *Trinity*,

Opinions Confuted.

nity, i. e. that there are in the Godhead Three Perſons, Father, Son and Holy Ghoſt; which is the Doctrin that our Saviour himſelf taught (and he taught it, that it might be *believed*) *Mat.* 28. 19. where the Celebration of *Baptiſm*, which is a ſolemn part of Divine Worſhip, is commanded to be *in the name of the Father, and of the Son, and of the Holy Ghoſt*, who are *One God*, 1 John 5. 7. *Theſe Three are One*, one Eſſence or Being, as the word "ἓν imports. Thoſe words of the Apoſtle are obſervable, 1 *Cor.* 1. 13. *Were ye baptiſed in the name of Paul?* As much as to ſay, *Baptiſm* is in the name of God, and not of a Man: Therefore when it is ſaid, *Go and Baptize in the name of the Father, Son, and Holy Ghoſt*, it is included, that theſe Three are *God*, *i. e.* Three Perſons of one and the ſame Deity. Thus it is manifeſt, that the believing of *Jeſus*'s being the *Meſſias*, or *Anointed* is not ſufficient to make a Man a Chriſtian Believer, but he muſt further believe theſe Propoſitions or Articles, *viz.* that the Son of God was made fleſh, *i. e.* aſſumed our Human Nature; that Chriſt is True God; that He with the Father and the Spirit are One God; for theſe are

are not only expressed in the *Gospels* and *Epistles* (out of both which we are to gather the Fundamental Articles of Faith) and consequently are to be assented to by all Christians, but the very Nature of the thing it self dictates that we ought to have a firm belief of these Truths; for otherwise when a Man professes his belief in the *Messias*, he is yet ignorant of the *Person* he pretends to believe in. He doth not know whether he believes in a *God* or in a *Man*, or to which of these he is beholding, for the Good he looks for by the Messias's coming. Now, Sir, you with your *Reasonableness of Christianity*, what do you think of this? Is it not reasonable that a Christian should (as the Apostle speaks of himself) *know whom he hath believed?* 2 Tim. 1. 12. Nay, is it not indispensably necessary, that he should know whether it be a *Divine*, or *Human*, or *Angelical* Power that he is obliged to, that so he may accordingly proportion his Affections and Service? for (what ever the late Set of Socinians hold) there must be a *difference* made between the Homage which is paid to a Creature (such as they declare Christ to be) and that which is due only to the Creator.

I will

Opinions Confuted. 13

I will refer the Reader to the Incomparable Bishop *Pearson* on the Second Article of the *Creed,* where he shews, the "*Necessity of our believing Christ to be the* "*Eternal Son of God, and God himself,* " 1. For the directing and confirming of "our Faith concerning the *Redemption* of "Mankind. 2. For the right informing "of us about that *Worship* and *Honour* "which are due to him. 3. For giving us "a right apprehension, and consequent- "ly a due value of the *Infinite Love* of "God the Father in sending his Only-be- "gotten Son into the World to die for "us. Thus this Judicious Writer. But our Nameless Author would perswade us, that there is no necessity of believing any such thing.

Then in the next place, we are to have a right conception concerning our *Recovery* and *Restauration* by this *Messias,* who is God-Man. And here those several Scriptures will furnish us with Articles, *As by the offence of one, judgment came upon all men to condemnation, even so by the righteousness of one the free gift came upon all men unto justification of life. For as by one mans disobedience many were made sinners, so by the obedience of one shall many be made righteous,* Rom. 5. 18, 19.

He

Some Late Socinian

He appeared to put away sin by the sacrifice of himself, Heb. 9. 26. *Christ was once offered to bear the sins of many,* Heb. 9.28. *Christ hath once suffered for sins, the just for the unjust,* 1 Pet. 3. 18. *He gave himself a Ransom for all men,* 1 Tim. 2.6. *Ye are redeemed with the precious blood of Christ,* 1 Pet. 1. 18, 19. And to it is prefix'd *ye know,* to let us understand that this Article is to be known and assented to. *We are bought with a price,* 1 Cor. 6. 20. and 7. 23. *We are reconciled unto God by the death of his Son,* Rom. 5. 10. *By him now we have received the Atonement,* v. 11. *By one offering he hath perfected for ever them that are sanctified,* Heb. 10. 14. *It behoved Christ to suffer, and to rise from the dead the third day,* Luk. 24. 46. *Christ must needs have suffered, and risen again from the dead,* Acts 17. 3. *He was taken up into heaven, and sat on the right hand of God,* Mark 16. 19. These and the like places afford us such Fundamental and Necessary Doctrins as these are, that by and for the Meritorious Righteousness and Obedience of Christ (the Second *Adam*) we are accounted Righteous and Obedient in the sight of God : That Christ was a Sacrifice for us, and suffered in our stead:

Opinions Confuted. 15

stead: That he satisfied Divine Justice by paying an Infinite Price for us; That by vertue of that Payment all the Debts, *i. e.* all the Sins of Believers are perfectly absolved: That hereby the anger of the Incensed Deity is pacified, and that we are entirely Reconciled to him: That we have an assurance of all this by Christ's rising from the dead, and ascending triumphantly into Heaven. These are *Principles of the Oracles of God*, Heb. 5. 12. These are part of the *Form of sound words*, 2 Tim. 1.13. which are indispensable Ingredients in the *Christian Faith*, which you may know by this, that if a man be obliged to the belief of the Messias's Coming, it is undeniably requisite that he should know *what* the Messias came to do for him, and that he should firmly yield assent to it. This I think no Man of Reason will deny: and then it will follow that these Articles which I have last mentioned are the Necessary and Unexceptionable object or matter of the Faith of a Christian Man. And here likewise it were easie to shew, that *Adoption, Justification, Pardon of Sins*, &c. which are Privileges and Benefits bestowed upon us by the *Messias*, are necessary matters of
our

our Belief, for we can't duly acknowledge him for our Benefactor and Saviour, unless we believe, that these Great Prerogatives are confer'd upon us.

Moreover, it is of undoubted necessity in order to our being *Christians*, that we know and believe what the *Messias requires of us*; which is contained in such general Texts as these, *That ye being delivered out of the hands of your enemies may serve him* (Christ our Deliverer) *without fear, in holiness and righteousness before him all the days of our life*, Luke 1. 75. *The grace of God which bringeth salvation, teacheth us, to deny ungodliness and worldly lusts*, &c. Tit. 2. 11, 12. *He gave himself for us, that he might reredeem us from all iniquity*, &c. Tit. 2. 14. *This is the will of God, even your sanctification*, 1 Thess. 4. 3. *Without Faith it is impossible to please God*, Heb. 11. 6. *Without holiness no man shall see the Lord*, Heb. 12. 14. Which places yield us such Propositions as these, that the *Messias* who vouchsafed to come into the World to redeem lost Man, requires of him universal Holiness and Righteousness, and the abandoning of all sin and ungodliness: That it was one grand end and design of Christ's visiting the World

Opinions Confuted. 17

would to redeem men from their iniquities, to sanctifie their Natures, and to make them entirely godly, sober and righteous in their Lives : That without these there is no Salvation, no Seeing of God in the regions of Glory, no hopes of Everlasting Happiness. The disbelieving of these *Articles* hath made so many Sorry *Christians* as we see every where, such as lay claim to that Honourable *Title*, but are regardless of that Holiness which should accompany it. We must not only believe that *Jesus is the Messias*, but we must believe this also that we can have no Benefit by this Messias unless we by Faith and Obedience adhere to him.

Neither is this enough, it is further matter of our Belief, as we are *Christians*, that our Salvation springs from the mere Favour and Bounty of God through his Son *Jesus Christ*, and that this is the only source of that Happiness which we expect. *By grace we are saved, through faith, and that not of our selves: it is the gift of God, Eph.* 2. 8. *Not by works of righteousness which we have done, but according to his Mercy he saveth us, Tit.* 3.5. Where there is not this perswasion and belief, the true notion of *Christianity* vanishes,

nishes, and the conceit of *Merit* comes in its room: Wherefore there is a Necessity that we believe and be perswaded aright as to this matter. We are Worthless Creatures of our selves, but there is a Worthiness derived to us from the Unspotted and Meritoriou Righteousness of him that is the Eternal Son of God. He that knows not this, he that believes not this deserves not the Name of a *Christian*. I should have been glad to have found something of this nature in this *Gentleman's Christianity*. But he endeavours to seduce his Readers by other apprehensions, he tells them that the bare assenting to this, that *Jesus is the Messias*, is the Summ Total of the Christian Faith, and the Gospel requires no more.

Lastly, The doctrines of the *Resurrection* of the *Final Judgment*, and of *Eternal Glory in heaven* are contained in such passages of the New Testament as these, *Christ will raise up his at the last day*, John 6. 44. *The Lord Jesus Christ shall judge the quick and the dead at his appearing*, 2 Tim. 4. 1. *Father, I will that they whom thou hast given me, be with me where I am, that they may behold my glory*, John 17. 24. And are not these Truths

Truths the proper Object of our *Faith* now under the Gospel, they so peculiarly belonging to the doctrine and belief of the *Messias*? Can we believe in him, and yet not believe these Great things which a e brought to light by his preaching the Gospel? For though they were in some measure discovered and revealed before (*i. e.* the General Doctrine concerning a Future State, and the Endless Happiness accompanying it was not unknown) yet *Christ*'s Words and those of the *Apostles* do more abundantly assure us of the truth of them: especially Christ's Rising from the dead and ascending into Glory have irrefragably confirmed the reality of them, according to that of St. *Peter, We are begotten again unto a lively hope by the resurrection of Jesus Christ from the dead, to an Inheritance incorruptible and undefiled, and that fadeth not away, reserved in heaven for us,* 1 *Pet.* 1. 4. Who but the *Vindicator* could imagine that these Evangelical Doctrines are *not Necessary Matter of Faith* to Christian Men? Who but he could fancy and (which is more) publickly assert that the belief of the *Messias*'s being sent from God, without being acquainted with his gracious appointment

pointment as to our *Future Rewards*, is all that is required as necessary to constitute a *Christian Believer*? Especially, when it is said, *He that comes unto God must believe that he is a Rewarder*, Heb. 11. 6. Observe it, *he must believe*: then it is not indifferent, but a *Necessary* Article of faith.

CHAP.

Opinions Confuted. 21

CHAP. II.

The foresaid Articles and Doctrines are proved to be Necessary *matter of* Christian Faith. *Not that a man is supposed* Actually *to exert his Assent and Belief every moment. That we may be True* Christians, All *these Fundamental Truths must be imbraced, and none excluded. The late Writer's* forgetfulness. *It is prov'd that he grounds his notion of* One Article *upon the Weakness of Understanding and Capacity in the Generality of people. Herein he follows the Steps of the* Racovians, *who submit the greatest Mysteries to the judgment of the Vulgar; and, if they will not bear that Test, reject them. The Doctrine of the* Trinity *how said to have no* Difficulty *in it. It contains in it no* Contradiction. *This Proposition,* Jesus is the Messias *is not more intelligible than any of the Articles before mentioned.*

THUS I have briefly set before the Reader those *Evangelical Truths,* those *Christian Principles* which belong to the very Essence of Christianity. I have proved them to be such, and I have

have reduced most of them to certain *Propositions*, which is a thing the *Vindicator* call'd for, *p.* 16. If what I have said will not content him, I am sure I can do nothing that will. And therefore, if he should capriciously require any thing more, it would be as great Folly in me to comply with it as it is in him to move it. From what I have said it is evident that he is grosly mistaken when he saith, *Whatever doctrines the Apostles required to be believed to make a man a Christian, are to be found in those places of Scripture which he hath quoted in his book, p.* 11. The places which he quotes are made use of by him to shew that there is but *One Article* of Belief, *viz.* that *Christ is the Messiah:* but I think I have sufficiently proved that there are Other Doctrines besides That which are requir'd to be believed to make a man a Christian. Why did the Apostles *write* these Doctrines? Was it not that those they writ to might give their *Assent* to them? Nay, did they not require Assent to them? Yes verily, for this is to be proved from the Nature of the things contained in those Doctrines, which were such as had *immediate* respect to the Occasion, Author, Way, Means, and

and Iſſue of their Redemption and Salvation, as any impartial judg by examining the ſeveral Particular Articles and Propoſitions will readily grant. So that the ſum of all amounts to this, The belief of thoſe things without the knowledg of which a man cannot be ſaved is abſolutely Neceſſary: but the belief of the foregoing Particulars is the belief of ſuch things without the knowledg of which a man cannot be ſaved; Therefore the belief of theſe Particulars is abſolutely neceſſary. None will be ſo refractory, I ſuppoſe, as to deny the firſt Propoſition in this Syllogiſm; therefore I am to prove the Second, which is eaſily effected thus. The belief of thoſe things which have *Immediate* reſpect to the Occaſion, Author, Way, Means, and Iſſue of our Salvation, and which are neceſſary for knowing the True Nature and Deſign of it, is the belief of ſuch things without the knowledg of which a man cannot be ſaved: but ſuch is the belief of the preceding Articles, *Ergo*.

Not without good reaſon therefore I call'd them the *Eſſential* and *Integral* Parts of our Chriſtian and Evangelical Faith: And why the *Vindicator* fleers at theſe Terms (*p.*18.) I know no reaſon but this that he can't confute the application of them. Surely none but this Upstart *Racovian* will have the confidence to deny that These Articles of Faith are such as are Necessary to constitute a *Christian*, as to the intellectual and doctrinal part of Christianity; such as must in some measure be known and assented to by him, such as must be generally receiv'd and imbrac'd by him. Not that a man is supposed every moment to *Actually* exert his Assent and Belief, for none of the Moral Vertues, none of the Evangelical Graces are exerted thus always. Wherefore, that Question, p. 16. (though he saith *he asks it seriously*) might have been spared, *Whether every one of these Fundamentals is required to be believed to make a Man a Christian, and such as without the Actual belief thereof, he cannot be saved?* Here is *Seriousness* pretended when there is none, for the design is only to Cavil, and (if he can) to expose my Assertion. But he is not able to do it, for all his Critical Demands are answered in these few words, *viz.* that the Intellectual (as well as the Moral) Endowments are never supposed to be Always in Act: they are exerted upon Occasion, and

not

not all of them at a time. And therefore he miſtakes if he thinks, or rather as he objects without thinking, that theſe Doctrines, if they be Fundamental and Neceſſary, muſt be *always actually* believed. No man beſides himſelf ever ſtarted ſuch a thing. And why ſhould not *every one* of theſe Evangelical Truths (which is another thing he puts into his Queſtion) be believed and imbraced? They are in our Bibles for that very purpoſe, as I have proved, and therefore I need not undertake it again here. Hence it follows that a man cannot be a *Chriſtian* without the knowledg and belief of theſe Truths which are the *baſis* of Religion, the Standard of the Chriſtian Faith, the very Badges and Characters of Chriſtianity. Wherefore for any man to make up Chriſtianity without the belief of theſe is a Ridiculous and abſurd attempt, and conſequently we may gueſs that none would have ventured upon it but this Writer. This is he that ſets up One Article *with defiance of the reſt*, (though he is much diſpleaſed with me for ſaying ſo, *p.* 31.) for what is excluding them wholly but *defying* them? Wherefore, ſeeing he utterly excludes all the reſt by

re-

representing them as *Useless to the making a man a Christian* (which is the design of his whole Undertaking) it is manifest that he *defies* them.

But let us hear what this Author pleads for himself. He founds his conceit of *One Article* partly upon this, that a Multitude of doctrines is obscure, and hard to be understood, and therefore he trusses all up in One Article, that the *poor people* and *bulk of mankind* may bear it. This is the Scope of a great part of his book. But his Memory doth not keep pace with his Invention, and thence he saith *he remembers nothing of this in his book. Vind.p.27.* This Worthy Writer doth not know his own Reasoning that he uses, as particularly thus, that he troubles Christian men with no more but *One Article*, because that is *Intelligible*, and all people high and low may comprehend it. For he hath chosen out (he thinks) a Plain and Easie Article, whereas the others which are commonly propounded are not generally agreed upon (he saith) and are dubious and uncertain. But the believing that *Jesus was the Messias* hath nothing of doubtfulness or obscurity in it. This the Reader will find to be the drift and
design

design of several of his Pages. And the reason why I did not quote any single one of them was because he insists on this so long together, and spins it out after his way. In *p.* 301. of his *Reasonableness of Christianity*, where he sets down the *short, plain, easie and intelligible Summary* (as he calls it) of Religion, couch'd in a Single Article, he immediately adds, *The All-merciful God seems herein to have consulted the poor of this world, and the bulk of mankind. These are Articles* (whereas he had set down but *One*) *that the labouring and illiterate man may comprehend.* He assigns this as a ground why it was God's pleasure there should be but One Point of Faith, because hereby Religion may be understood the better, the generality of people may comprehend it. This he represents as a Great Kindness done by God to men, whereas a Variety of Articles would be hard to be understood. This he enlarges upon, and flourishes it over after his fashion, and yet *he desires to know when he said so, p.* 29. *Vindic.*

Good Sir, let me be permitted to acquaint you that your Memory is as defective as your Judgment; for in the very *Vindication* you attribute it to *the goodness*

ness and condescention of the Almighty that he requires nothing as absolutely necessary to be believed but what is suited to Vulgar capacities and the comprehensions of illiterate men, p. 30. It is clear then that you found your *One Article* on this, that it is suited to *Vulgar capacities,* whereas the Other Articles mentioned by me are obscure and ambiguous, and therefore surpass the comprehension of the Illiterate. And yet you pretend that you have forgot that any such thing was said by you: which shews that you are Careless of your Words, and that you forget what you write. What shall we say to such an Oblivious Author as this? He takes no notice of what falls from his own pen, and therefore within a page or two he confutes himself, and gives himself the Lye.

The plain truth is, he *Socinianizes* here, but will not own it, which makes him run into these Contradictions. He follows the steps of his Good Patron *Crellius* (one of the stiffest *Racovians* that we have) who throws aside several Articles of faith because they are Dark and Difficult, and not adapted to the Capacity of the Vulgar. This very thing he alledges to set off his Arguments against

the

Opinions Confuted. 29

the Holy *Trinity*, *viz*. that * the doctrine which he maintains is *according to the understanding of the Vulgar*. *The Common people* (he faith) *among the Jews, the Fishermen did not apprehend the doctrine of Three Persons in the Deity: neither do the Vulgar Christians at this day form any such notion*: therefore away with the doctrine of the *Trinity*. And this is the guise and practice of our *Socinians* at this day: it is known that they are wont to propound this Sacred Point to the very School-boys (very great Judges indeed) and to demand their Resolution of it, and they pretend that they give it in the Negative. All the appeal now is to *Vulgar Capacities*, to the judgment of the *Multitude*. If these please to allow of any more Articles of Belief than One, then our Author will consent to it that we shall have them: but he acquaints us that *they* are for no more but *One*, and therefore we must be content with That. This is his New *Divinity*. And a † *Socinian* Brother, who undertakes the defence of his Notions, seconds him in this, telling us that

the

---

* *De Uno Deo Patre. l.1.c. 1.* † The Exceptions of Mr. *E. &c.* examined.

the Articles of faith which are generally propounded by *Divines* are *difficult, obscure, unintelligible, abstruse,* but the One Article of Mr. Lock) *is not so,* but is exactly calculated for the Vulgar Meridian, and therefore is the only Authentick and Necessary Point in the Christian Theology.

I think the Reader will bear me witness that I have refuted this wild Conceit by giving a distinct account of the Evangelical Doctrines and Articles before mentioned, and at the same time shewing how Intelligible and Plain they are, and by letting him see the Absolute Necessity of their being assented to and embraced by every Christian. No true Lover of God and Truth need *doubt* of any of them, for there is no Ambiguity and Doubtfulness in them. They shine with their own light, and to an unprejudiced eye are plain, evident and illustrious. And they would always continue so if some Ill-minded men did not perplex and entangle them, on purpose to render them contemptible, yea, to exclude them wholly from being the matter of our belief. And as to the doctrine of the *Trinity,* which is the Main Verity which these men set themselves against,

against, there is not any Difficulty, much less any Absurdity or Contradiction (as they are wont to cry out) in that Article of our Christian Belief. Indeed there is a *Difficulty* in this and several Other Truths of the Gospel as to the *Exact Manner* of the things themselves, which we shall never be able to comprehend, at least not on this side of Heaven: but there is *no Difficulty* as to the Reality and Certainty of them, because we know they are Revealed to us by God in the Holy Scriptures. Nay, as to the thing it self, thus far we can apprehend that it is not impossible or absurd that the Three Distinct Persons in the Deity should be One God, for there may be a Plurality of Persons in the same Infinite Essence. Every Person doth not require a Single Particular Essence, or if they will call the Three Numerical Subsistencies by the name of *Essences*, yet they are united in One General *Substance* or *Essence*, which is common to them all. And when they say it is a *Contradiction* that One should be Three, which is as much as to say, One is not One, this is soon taken off by replying (and that most truly) that *One and not One* in the *same respect* is a Contradiction, but *One and*

not

not One in *different respects* is no Contradiction. Any smatterer in Logick knows this. And this is the case here, for tho the Three Personalities be distinguish'd, and that really, yet they agree in One Common Essence, and so the Divinity is both *One* and *Three* in different respects, on different considerations. And this is that which is abundantly testified in Scripture, in the *Gospels* as well as the *Epistles* (let our Author remember that:) there we learn that the Divine Essence or Nature is branch'd out into Three Distinct Persons,* *Father, Son* and *Holy Ghost*, and that * *these Three are One.*

Then as to the Proposition which this New Modeller of Christianity commends to the World as the only Necessary Matter of Faith. although he pretends it is more Intelligible than any of those that I have named, yet any Judicious Man cannot but see the contrary, for this must be explain'd (as well as those) before his *Vulgar Capacities* can apprehend it. Here first the name *Jesus*, which is of Hebrew Extraction, though since Greciz'd, must be expounded, and so must the Word *Messias* (as I said before:)

---

* *Mat.* 28. 19. *John* 10. 30.

fore:) And when this is done they must be told, even according to the confession of a late * Socinian Writer (whom afterwards I must discourse with a little) *the manner of his being the Messiah, such as being conceived by the Holy Ghost and Power of the most High, his being anointed with the Holy Ghost, his being raised from the dead, and exalted to be a Prince and a Saviour.* And then they must be told for what End and Purpose this was (or else they can have no true belief of the *Messias*) under which several Weighty Truths are comprehended. And if he doth not agree to this, *viz.* that the Words must be thus *Opened* and *Explained*, and fully understood so that Christian Souls may have the true sense of them, then he doth as good as say that the bare pronouncing of these Words *Jesus is the Messias* is enough to make a Christian. And we shall be apt to think that he intends this for a *Charm* or *Spell*, and that the very Syllables will suffice to make one a True Believer, especially if he be one of the *Vulgar* and *Illiterate*. But it may be he hath something else to say to an *Other* Rank of Men: Perhaps he

---

* The Exceptions, &c. examined.

he holds that there is one Christianity for the *bulk of mankind*, and another for the Finer and Better Sort of People: And then it is likely he will tell us of two Heavens, one very Spacious to hold the *Multitude*, and the other of a Lesser Compass to receive the rest. These are the Absurdities (which I confess I delight not in exposing or so much as mentioning) that this New Notion may produce. Whence it appears that all his jargon and chatter about his *One Article* are vain and insignificant, and are serviceable only to gull the Unwary Reader, and (which is worse) to debauch Christianity it self.

CHAP.

CHAP. III.

The late Writer's passing by the Epistles, *and not collecting any Articles of Faith out of them shew his* Contempt *of them. His Evasion,* viz. *that the* Epistles *were writ to those who were already* Believers, *is proved to be groundless. If it were true, it is nothing to his purpose. The* Epistles *teach Fundamentals. His other Evasion,* viz. *that* the Fundamental Articles in the Epistles are mixed without distinction with other Truths *discovered to be of no force, and Retorted upon him. The true Reason why he went no further than the* Gospels *and the* Acts. *His other Excuses for rejecting the doctrines contained in the* Epistles *examined, and found to be Sophistical. He travels as far as* China *for* Prudence, *and there borrows it of the* Missionary Jesuites. *The* Rom. 14. 1. *which he alledges, authorizes him not to impose upon* Weak Christians. *His Evasions are inconsistent with themselves, and accordingly not well approved of by the Party. His Objection about the* Apostles Creed *fully answered.* Our Church's Judgment

Some Late Socinian

concerning the Articles of this Creed. This Profession of Faith hath several Articles in it which Socinians *will not subscribe to. Whilest he is censuring, he commits a great* Blunder. *He mistakes and misrepresents the Gospel-Dispensation.*

BUT the Gentleman is not without his *Evasions*, and he sees it is high time to make use of them. This puts him into some disorder, for when he comes to speak of my mentioning his ill treatment of the *Epistles* (which he purposely omitted when he made his Collection of Articles, or rather when after all his search he found but One Article) you may observe that he begins to grow Warmer than before. Now this Meek Man is nettled, and you may perceive that he is sensible of the Scandal that he hath given to good people by his slighting of the *Epistolary* Writings of the Holy Apostles: yet he is so cunning as to disguise his Passion as well as he can. He *requires me to publish to the World those passages which shew his Contempt of the Epistles, p.* 19. But what need I, Good Sir, do this, when you have done it your self? I appeal to the Reader whether

ther (after your tedious Collections out of the *Four Evangelists*) your passing by the *Epistles*, and neglecting wholly what the Apostles say in them be not *publishing to the World your Contempt of them*.

But let us hear why he did not attempt to collect any Articles out of these Writings: he assigns this as One Reason, *The Epistles being writ to those who were already Believers, it could not be supposed that they were writ to them to teach them Fundamentals, p.* 13, 14. *Vindic.* Certainly no man could have conjectured that he would have used such an Evasion as this. I will say that for him, he goes beyond all Surmises, he is above all Conjectures: he hath a faculty of Shifting which no creature on Earth can ever fathom. Do we not know that the *Four Gospels* were Writ to and for *Believers* as well as *Unbelievers*? Are we not particularly and expresly told by St. *Luke* that *he writ his Gospel to the most Excellent Theophilus? Luk.* 1. 3. whom all grant to be a *Believing Christian* of some eminent rank. Or if this Author be so singular as to question it, he may be satisfied in *v.* 4. by the Evangelist himself. And so the *Acts* of the Apostles we find are dedicated to the same Eminent Believer, *Acts* 1. 1. By the same Argument then that he would perswade us that the *Fundamentals* are not to be sought for in the *Epistles*, we may prove that they were not to be sought for in the *Gospels*, and in the *Acts*, for even these were writ to those that *believed*. And yet it is clear that this Writer did not make use of this Argument, otherwise he would not have confined the Fundamentals to the *Gospels* and the *Acts*. Here then is want of Sincerity in a great measure, which hath been accounted heretofore a good qualification in a Writer.

Again, granting that the *Epistles* were all of them writ to those that *already believed*, yet what can this be to his purpose? Must no *Believers* have any *Fundamentals* taught them? What is the meaning then of 1 *John* 2. 21. *I have not written unto you because you know not the Truth, but because you know it.* Suppose they have *forgot* the Fundamentals, or have *corrupted* and perverted them? as was the case of the *Galatians*, who mixed the Law with the Gospel, Legal Works with Faith; and of the Dispersed *Hebrews* who had received the Christian Doctrine, but were falling away

from

Opinions Confuted.

from it. Might not the Apoſtle, yea did he not in his *Epiſtles* to theſe Perſons remind them of the *Great Articles of the Chriſtian Faith?* Did he not, when he writ to the *Galatians* aſſert the doctrine of Juſtification through faith in Chriſt's Righteouſneſs, without the Works of the Law? Did he not in his Epiſtle to the Wavering *Hebrews* endeavour to eſtabliſh them in Chriſtianity by diſplaying the Excellency and Tranſcendency of the *Prieſthood* of Chriſt, by convincing them of the Efficacy and Perfection of the *One Sacrifice* of the Meſſias on the Croſs, whereby the ſins of mankind are perfectly Expiated? So *St. John's firſt Epiſtle* was written on occaſion of the Chriſtian Churches (converted from Judaiſm) being endanger'd by certain Seducers that were crept in among them, and labour'd to unſettle their belief concerning the *Divinity* as well as the Humanity of our Saviour. Whereupon this Apoſtle, who had clearly delivered the doctrine of the *Holy Trinity* in the beginning of his *Goſpel*, now more eſpecially urges that Principal Article of their Faith the *Deity* of Chriſt, *chap. 2. v.* 22, 23. and alſo in expreſs words aſſerts the *Whole Trinity*, *chap.* 5. *v.* 7. Thus it is manifeſt that the Apostles in their *Epistles* taught *Fundamentals*, which is contrary to what this Gentleman faith, that such a thing *could not be supposed*: and he would pretend That as a reason why he did not look for any Necessary Articles of Faith in the *Epistles*. But we see how groundless his pretence is.

Hear another feigned ground of his omitting the *Epistles*, viz. *because the Fundamental Articles are here promiscuously, and without distinction mix'd with other Truth.* p. 14. But who sees not that this is a mere Elusion? for on the same account he might have forborn to search for Fundamental Articles in the *Gospels*, for they do not lie there together, but are dispersed up and down: the Doctrinal and Historical part are mix'd with one another: but he pretends to sever them; why then did he not make a separation between the Doctrines in the *Epistles* and those Other Matters that are treated of there? He hath nothing to reply to this, and therefore we must again look upon what he hath suggested as a cast of his Shuffling faculty. Or if he should excuse himself by saying that Necessary and Fundamental Principles can't be distinguish'd from

those

Opinions Confuted. 41

those other Truths which occur in the Epistolary Writings, any one may discover the insufficiency of such a plea, because Necessary Truths may be distinguish'd from those that are not such by the Nature and High Importance of them, by their Immediate respect to the Author and Means of our Salvation.

Besides, I suppose this Flourishing *Scribler* (he knows very well why I give him that particular Title) will not deny that the *Epistles* contain divers Rules of Holy Living, several Religious Precepts in order to the practise of Godliness; and that these are not so *promiscuously and without distinction mixt with other Truths* but that they may easily be distinguish'd from them. Why then may we not expect to find *Necessary Doctrines of Faith* in these Writings as well as Instructions concerning the practise of Holiness, and the regulating of our Lives? And why may we not distinguish between these and the Occasional Matters as well as between the Others and them? Nay, it is certain that those Necessary doctrines of Faith which were but lightly touch'd upon in the *Gospels* and the *Acts* are distinctly and fully explain'd in these *Epistles*. The truth then is that

the

the Gentleman was loth to go any further than the former: these latter affrighted him, for he knew either by reading them or by hear-say, that there were several *Other Divine Truths* in them, which have been generally thought to be Necessary to be believ'd in order to making a man a Christian; but our Author had no kindness for them. He commands his Readers not to stir a jot further than the *Acts*. *It is not in the Epistles,* faith he, *that we are to learn what are the Fundamental Articles of faith,* p. 295. *They were written for resolving of doubts and reforming of mistakes,* (as he faith in the same place) and therefore I forbid you to seek for *Fundamental doctrines* there, you will but lose your labour, and moreover you will meet in these Writings with several Points which we approve not of, and therefore must not admit of, because *Faustus Socinus* hath given us a charge to the contrary.

But let us hear further what this *Vindicator* faith to excuse his rejection of the Doctrines contain'd in the *Epistles,* and his putting us off with One Article of Faith. *What if the Author* (meaning himself) *design'd his Treatise, as the Title shews, chiefly for those who were not yet*

throughly

throughly or firmly Chriſtians : purpoſing to work upon thoſe who either wholly disbeliev'd or doubted of the Truth of the Chriſtian Religion? p. 6. Here he comes with his *what if's*, and gives another palpable proof of Counterfeiting, and that in Religion. Now, ſeeing his Book is ſifted, and the deſign of it is laid open, he would make us believe that he intended his Piece for *Atheiſts, Turks, Jews* and *Pagans*, and a few Weak Chriſtians; for theſe he muſt mean by thoſe that *wholly disbelieve*, and thoſe that are *not firmly Chriſtians*. And he would bring in his *Title* to ſpeak for him, but it ſaith not a word in his behalf; for how thoſe that wholly diſregard and *disbelieve the Scriptures* of the New Teſtament, (as Gentiles, Jews, Mahometans and all Atheiſts do) are like to attend to the *Reaſonableneſs of Chriſtianity as deliver'd in the Scripture* is not to be conceived, and therefore we look upon all this as mere Sham and Sophiſtry. He is put hard to it, and like one a drowning he faſtens on any thing next at hand. That is his caſe, as any man may perceive. But I ask, Why had we not a hint (one gentle hint at leaſt) of this in all his Book? It would have been very uſeful to the Reader to have been acquainted with his Design. No: he thinks otherwise, for in the same Page he saith, *Would any one blame his Prudence if he mention'd only those Advantages,* (viz. of Christ's Coming) *which all Christians* (especially *Socinian Christians*) *are agreed in*? He hath bethought himself better since he first publish'd his Notions, and (as the result of that) he now begins to resolve what he writ into *Prudence*. I know whence he had this Method (and 'tis likely he hath taken more than this from the same hands) viz. from the Missionary *Jesuites* that went to preach the Gospel to the people of *China*. We are told that they instructed them in some matters relating to our *Saviour*; they let them know that *Jesus* was the *Messias*, the Person promised to be sent into the World, but they conceal'd his *Sufferings* and *Death* and they would not let them know any thing of his *Passion* and *Crucifixion*. So our Author (their humble Imitator) undertakes to instruct the World in Christianity with an omission of its *Principal Articles,* and more especially that of the *Advantage* we have by *Christ's Death*, which was the Prime thing design'd in his Coming into the world.

Opinions Confuted. 45

world. This he calls *Prudence* · so that to hide from the people the Main Articles of the Christian Religion, to disguise the Faith of the Gospel, to betray Christianity it self, is according to this Excellent Writer the Cardinal Vertue of *Prudence.* May we be deliver'd then, say I, from a *Prudential Racovian.*

He would clear himself by quoting *Rom.* 14. 1. *Him that is weak in the faith receive ye, p.·7.* as if that Text authorized him to deceive Novices and Weak Christians; as if because they are Infirm, therefore he must Strengthen them by Imposing upon them. It may be he will say, *Children* must have but few Lessons given them: but I answer, there is difference between *few* and *only One* ; and there is difference between telling them that there is but One, and afterwards hinting that there are More. For that must be the meaning of his *What if he design'd his Treatise chiefly for those,* &c. What if he first of all tells them that nothing is absolutely requisite to be believed but this that *Jesus is the Messias,* and what if afterwards he intends to let them know that something else is requir'd of them? And yet at the same time (such is the unaccountable
humour

humour of the Gentleman) he declares that Nothing more is requir'd of them. Here is no bottom for any thing he faith. He contradicts himself, and imposes falsities upon mens minds. He would in one place (I remember) fancifully please himself by thinking that *all his sins which I espie in his book are sins of Omission, p.* 9. But if this be not one of *Commission* (and that a very Great one) it is hard to tell what is. He pretends a *Design of his Book* which was never so much as thought of till he was follicited by his brethren to vindicate it. But now, (see how his *Pious Frauds* prosper) when he hath attempted it, they are displeased with the way he hath taken. And no wonder, because they cannot but perceive that his *Vindication* is inconsistent with his *Treatise,* and that by these last Evasions and Collusions he hath in a great measure betray'd *their* Cause, as well as that of *Christianity.* I find that they have only this to excuse him that he did not take Time enough to consider of what he Writ: but for my part, I think that adds to his Fault.

But this Author of the *New Christianity* wisely objects that the *Apostle's Creed* hath none of these Articles and Doctrines
which

Opinions Confuted. 47

which I mentioned, *p.* 12, 13. Nor doth any confiderate man wonder at it, for the *Creed* is a Form of outward Profeffion which is *chiefly* to be made in the Publick Affemblies, when Prayers are put up by the Church, and the Holy Scriptures are read. Then this *Abriagment* of Faith is properly ufed, or when there is not generally time or opportunity to make any Enlargement. But we are not to think that it *exprefly* contains in it all the Neceffary and Weighty Points, all the Important Doctrines of our Belief, it being only defign'd to be an *Abstract.* It is with this *Creed* as 'tis with the *Commandments* and the *Lord's Prayer*. If a man *doth* not more than is exprefly enjoyned in the *Decalogue*, he can't be faid to *Act* as a Chriftian. If he *prays* for no more than is exprefly mentioned in the Petitions of the forefaid *Prayer* he can't be faid to *Pray* as a Good Chriftian. So if a man *believe* no more than is in *exprefs* terms in the *Apoftle's Creed*, his Faith will not be the *Faith* of a Chriftian. And yet ftill it is to be granted that as all things to be *done* and all things to be *prayed for* are *reducible* to the Ten Commandments and the Lord's Prayer, fo All matters of Faith in fome manner

manner may be *reduced* to this Brief Platform of Belief. But when I call it an *Abstract* or *Abbreviature*, it is implied that there are more Truths to be known and assented to by a Christian, in order to making him really so, than what we meet with here.

And yet I must take leave to tell our *Vindicator* that this *Creed* hath more in it than he and his brethren will subscribe to. If he were not above *Catechisms* as well as *Creeds*, I might remind him of *Our Church*'s judgment concerning the Articles of this *Creed*. *Qu. What dost thou chiefly learn in these Articles of thy Belief? Answ. First, I learn to believe in God the Father, who had made me and all the world: Secondly, in God the Son, who hath redeemed me and all mankind: Thirdly, in God the Holy Ghost, who sanctifieth me and all the Elect People of God?* These are killing words to a Disciple of *Socinus*, who acknowledges neither the God-head of the *Son*, nor of the *Holy Ghost*, nor the *Redemption* or *Sanctification* by either. Yet our Church, with all the Christian Churches in the world, owns these Truths to be contained in the *Apostles Creed*. And there are other Articles of this Symbol (let them palliate it as they please)

Opinions Confuted.

pleafe,) which the *Racovian* Gentlemen are unwilling to give their affent to They faulter about Chrift's *Judging the quick and the dead*, they partly deny the *Refurrection of the body*, they deny *Life Everlafting* as it refpects wicked men, for they hold that thefe fhall be Annihilated, of all which I may have occafion to fpeak another time. At prefent I only take notice of their lopping off feveral Articles from this *Creed*.

But was it not judicioufly faid by this Writer that *it is well for the Compilers of the Creed that they lived not in my days? p. 12.* I tell you, Friend, it was impoffible they fhould, for the Learned * *Ufher* and † *Voffius* and others have proved that that *Symbol* was drawn up not at once, but that fome Articles of it were adjoyned many years after, far beyond the extent of any man's life; and therefore the Compilers of the Creed could not live in my days, nor could I live in theirs: but I let this pafs as one of the *blunders* of our Thoughtful and Mufing Author. Nor had he reafon to think

---

* Diatr. de Symbol. † D: Trib. Symb.

think that thofe that made the Apoftles Creed would have been cenfured by me, for I have vindicated and afferted their *Articles*, whereas he and his friends have new-modell'd the *Creed*, yea indeed have prefented us with One Article inftead of Twelve, and in order to that have funk the *Epiftles*, becaufe they are not *Socinianized, all over Socinianized*.

If this Gentleman had faid that the belief of *Jefus*'s being the *Meffias* was one of the firft and leading acts of Chriftian Faith, he had faid right, and none would have oppofed it. If he had faid that the knowledg of the Gofpel, and confequently of the Doctrines of it, advanc'd at firft by degrees, and fhone brighter after our Saviour's Afcenfion than before, he had fpoken truth ; but when he pofitively and peremptorily declares that neither at firft nor afterwards there was any Neceffity of believing more than this that *Jefus is the Meffias*, he mifreprefents the Gofpel-Difpenfation, and miftakes the nature of Chriftiaanity. To ftop here, and go no further is unfufferable. This is as if a *Breeder up of Children and Youth* fhould carry them

no

no further than the A B C. He is wholly for *reducing* of Christianity, whereas he should have given it in its Full and Ample Extent; especially he should not have kept back any thing of the *Foundation*.

Some Late Socinian

CHAP. IV.

The Christian Faith *which this Gentleman describes is of the same scantling with that of the* Mahometans. *The Affinity between the* Turks *and* Anti-trinitarians. *The* Devils *are capable of a higher degree of Faith than that which he saith makes a* Christian. *A brief Idea of the Compleat Faith of a Christian. The Danger of asserting that there is but* One Article *of Christian belief necessary to be assented to. This is the way to introduce* Darkness *and* Blindness *into* Christendom, *and to promote the designs of that Church which cherishes* Ignorance *as the Mother of Devotion and Religion. How far this Writer is instrumental in it. What care he hath of mens* Souls, *and of their* Salvation. *It is the practise of* Socinian *Writers to curtail Christianity, and to cut off as many Fundamental Articles from it as they can. This Writer had his Platform from* Crellius. *He is approved of and applauded by the* English Socinians. *Three Reasons assign'd why the* Socinians *agree to maim the Heads of Christianity, and to reduce all into One Article. The Office of* Catechizing

Opinions Confuted. 53

techizing *was not instituted for the teaching of* One *Article of Faith only.*

IT is likely I shall further exasperate this Author when I desire the Reader to observe that this *Lank Faith* of his is in a manner no other than the *Faith of a Turk.* For the * Alcoran acknowledges that the *Spirit of God bore witness to Christ the Son of* Mary : *a Divine Soul was put into him. He was the Messenger of the Spirit, and the Word of God.* And in another place *God* is brought in declaring that *he had sent Christ the Son of* Mary, &c. And in other places he is mention'd as a *Prophet*, as a *Great Man*, one Commission'd by God, and *sent by him* into the world. This is of the like import with what our good *Ottoman* Writer the *Vindicator* saith of our Saviour, and this he holds is the sum of all that is Necessary to be believ'd concerning him. The *Mahometans* call themselves *Musselmen*, or rather (according to the true account of the *Arabick* word) † *Moslemim*, i. e. *Believers*; and what difference is there between

E 3

---

* Azoar 1. * Azoar 67. † From the Arabick verb *islam, credidit*, whence the Mahometan Religion is call'd *Islamismus.*

tween one of them and our Author's *Believer?* The former believes that Christ is a Good Man, and not above the nature of a Man, and sent of God to give Instructions to the world: and the Faith of the latter is of the very same scantling. Thus he confounds *Turky* with *Christendom*; and those that have been reckon'd as *Infidels* are with him *Christians*. He seems to have consulted the *Mahometan Bible*, which faith, * *Christ did not suffer on the cross, did not die* ; for he and his Allies speak as meanly of *these Articles* as if there were no such thing. The Alcoran often talks (particularly see the *Last Chapter* of it) against Christ's being *the Son of God by Generation.* It is one of the First Principles of *Mahometism* that there is but *One God neither begetting nor begot.* See *Sulburgius*'s *Saracenica.* This is it which our Author drives at when he labours to prove the *Messias* and *the Son of God* are terms synonymous, as you shall hear by and by. This reminds me of that Affinity and Correspondence which hath been between the *Turks* and this Gentleman's Party. † *Servetus* conferr'd notes with the *Alcoran,* when he

un-

---

* Alcor. Azoar. 11 † De Trin. l. 1.

Opinions Confuted. 55

undertook to fetch an Argument out of it to difprove the *Deity* of our Saviour. It is obfervable that thofe Countreys of *Europe* which border on the *Sultan*'s dominions, as *Hungary*, *Tranfilvania*, &c. abound with *Socinians* and *Antitrinitarians*. The inhabitants of thefe places accommodate themfelves to their Potent Neighbours, they make fome approach to the *Conquerer's Creed*. Some of thefe men have lately got footing in *England*, and becaufe they and the *Great Turk* difbelieve the *Trinity*, therefore we muft all be Profelytes to their opinion. They are making way for this by taking away all the Articles of the Chriftian Faith but One. And our late Writer is the Inftrument they make ufe of for this purpofe. This Great Mufti hath given us a Hopeful Draught of *Chriftianity*; and it was fit the Englifh Reader fhould know that a *Turk* according to him is a *Chriftian*, for he makes the fame Faith ferve them both.

Nay, in the laft place, let us take notice that this Gentleman prefents the world with a very Ill notion of *Faith*, for the very *Devils* are capable of all that *Faith* which he faith makes a *Chriftian man*, yea of more, for we read that
they

they *believed Jesus to be the Son of God*, Mat. 8. 29. They cried out to him, *Thou art Christ the Son of God*, Luke 4. 41. which latter words in both places denote his *Divinity*, as I shall shew afterwards. But besides this *Historical Faith* (as it is generally call'd by Divines) which is giving credit to Evangelical Truths as barely reveal'd, there must be something else added to make up the True Substantial Faith of a *Christian*. With the Assent of the Understanding must be joyn'd the Consent or Approbation of the Will. All those Divine Truths which the Intellect assents to must be allow'd of by this Elective power of the Soul. True Evangelical Faith is a hearty Accepting of the Messias as he is offer'd in the Gospel. It is a sincere and impartial submission to all things requir'd by the *Evangelical Law*, which is contain'd in the *Epistles* as well as the *other Writings*. And to this Practical Assent and Choice there must be added likewise a firm Trust and Reliance in the Blessed Author of our Salvation. But this late Undertaker, who attempted to give us a more perfect account than ever was before of *Christianity as it is deliver'd in the Scriptures*, brings us no tidings of any such

Faith

Opinions Confuted.

Faith belonging to *Christianity*, or discover'd to us in the *Scriptures.* Which gives us to understand that he verily believes there is no such *Christian Faith,* for in some of his Numerous Pages (especially 191, 192, &c.) where he speaks so much of *Belief* and *Faith,* he might have taken occasion to insert *one word* about this Compleat Faith of the Gospel.

Having thus represented how *Defective,* how *Narrow,* how *Erroneous,* how *Mistaken* this Unknown Writer's *Christianity,* and especially his *Faith* is; I will now proceed to shew how *Dangerous* and *Pernicious* this sort of Doctrine is. Here is a Contrivance set up for the bringing in of *Darkness* and *Barbarism* into the Christian world. The only Necessary Point of Belief that the *Old Testament* delivers, is, according to these Gentlemen, that *there is One God:* and all the *New Testament* affords us as matter of Necessary Faith is this, that *Jesus is the Messias.* Carry but these Two Articles along with you, and you are a True Christian. There is no *Necessity* at all of being acquainted with the Reveal'd Doctrine concerning the Cause of Mankinds Degeneracy and Corruption, which gave occasion to the *Messias's* Coming into the world.

world. There is no Necessity of knowing whether this *Messias* be God or Man, or both: there is no Necessity of understanding whether he came to suffer and dye in our stead, and to satisfie the Divine Justice, and to purchase Salvation for us by his Blood: There is no Necessity of believing that without Faith and Evangelical Obedience we cannot have any Benefit by the Messias: There is no Necessity of being perswaded that our Salvation springs from the mere Grace and Bounty of Heaven: There is no Necessity of believing the Privileges and Rewards (both here and hereafter) which are entail'd on Christianity. There is but a *Single Article of Belief*, and this is a very Short one too, *viz.* that *Jesus is the Messias*; and if you assent to This you are as *Sound a Christian* and as *Good a Believer* as this Gentleman can make you. One would think that seeing there are so many Branches of the Evangelical Faith commended to us and urged upon us by the Apostles in their Epistles (some of which our Saviour himself in the Gospel, had made mention of) one would think, I say, that a man that hath a True Sense of Christianity, and is a Lover of Souls should endeavour

deavour to display before the world these Several Parts of the *Christian Belief*, and should be earnest with men to embrace them All, and not to omit or neglect any of them, seeing they all so nearly concern their Everlasting Wellfare. But here comes One that makes it his great business to beat men off from taking notice of these Divine Truths, he represents them as wholly Unnecessary to be believed, he cries down all Articles of Christian Faith but One. He at this time of day, when *Christianity* is so bright, strives to darken and eclipse it; he hides it from the faces of mankind, draws a thick Veil over it, will not suffer them to look into it, takes the Holy and Inspired *Epistles* (which are as much the Word of God as the *Gospels*) out of their way, and tells them again and again that a *Christian man* or *Member of Christ* need not know or believe any more than that One Individual Point which he mentions.

Hear O ye Heavens, and give ear O Earth, judg whether this be not the way to introduce *Darkness* and *Ignorance* into Christendom, whether this be not blinding of mens eyes, and depriving them of that Blessed Light which the
Writings

Writings of the Evangelists and Apostles should illuminate mens minds with. Which makes me think sometimes (and perhaps the Reader doth so too) that this Writer and the other Confederates are Under-hand-Factors for that Communion (though they would seem to be much against it) which cries up *Ignorance* as the mother of Devotion and Religion. If they had not some such design, why do they labour so industriously to keep the people in Ignorance, to tell them that One Article is enough for them, and that there is no *Necessity* of knowing any other doctrines of the Bible? Thus by following their *Italian* Master *Socinus*, they trade for that *Countrey*. And this *Vindicator* among the rest trafficks very visibly for it whilest he blasteth so substantial a part of the New Testament as the *Epistolary* Writings are. Would not one be apt to suspect that (as their *Roman* Masters have done) they would afterwards not only keep a part, but the Whole Scripture from the people? And so we shall travel to *Rome* by the way of *Racovia*.

And here you may see now what his Pretences of Love to *the bulk of mankind* come to. See how Sincere he

Opinions Confuted.

is in taking care of the *Salvation of their Souls*, which is a thing that he more than once mentions, and with some reflection (*p. 9. Vindicat.*) on me as if I disregarded that Great Concern. But I hope I have in some measure faithfully discharged that part, though the *Great Judg* of heaven and earth knows my manifold deficiencies and failings in it; but I am well satisfied that this Inferior Inquisitor cannot charge me with a neglect in that Great and Important Work, which I have made the business of my life. But behold how this Censorious Gentleman himself manifests his regard to the *Salvation of peoples Souls* when he puts out their Eyes, when he studies how to nurse them up in Ignorance and Blindness, and thereby to Ruine their Souls for ever. He can afford them but One Article out of the Whole New Testament. That must suffice them now, and perhaps afterwards it will be thought too much.

Here, before I proceed any further, I would take notice that the Project of the Necessity of but One Article of Christian Belief is the direct Spawn and Product of *Socinianism*, but improved by this Author. He that hath convers'd with the

Unitarian Writers is fenfible how they endeavour to cramp our Belief and Knowledg, and cut off as many Fundamental Articles of Religion as they can. * They infift upon this, that the Points neceffary to be known are but *Few :* they interpret thofe places of Scripture which directly fpeak of *Knowing of God, i.e.* of knowing his Nature and Attributes, and other matters in Religion that are to be believed, concerning a *Practical Knowledg.* * *Socinus* leads the way, undervaluing the former fort of Knowledg, and interpreting *Acts* 17. 27. *feeking the Lord, if haply they may feel after him, and find him,* concerning a Holy Life ; whereas the plain fcope of the place will convince any unprejudiced man that it is fpoken of thofe who being ignorant of God, labour to throw off that Ignorance, and to attain to a Knowledg of him, in order to their right worfhiping and ferving him. The reft follow this Ring-leader, and accordingly you may obferve that in their *Definitions* of *Religion* they feldom (or never) infert *Knowledg* as any part of it, but they wholly define it to be a Living according
to

---

* Socin. de Cognit. Dei. Oftorod..Inftit. cap. 3, ✢ Epifcop. Apol. Remonftr. ' Prælect. cap. 5.

to the Divine Precepts and Promises, or to be the Way to Eternal Life and Happiness. Some of them seem to restrain that place, *John* 17.3. *that they might know thee the only true God*, &c. unto a Practical Knowledg. And in other particulars it might be shewed that they very much disparage the *Doctrinal* Part of Christianity, and more especially take care to abbreviate and cut off the Fundamentals of it. *Crellius* is much for diminishing and reducing the knowledg and belief of the Articles of Faith. *The Sacred Writers* (saith * he) *when they speak of that knowledg in which Religion, or the way to eternal life consists, speak not of that knowledg whereby any Attribute that is Essential to God or Christ is known.* Here is the Platform of our Gentleman's Design, and thence let the Reader guess whose part he takes. *Crellius* hath given him his Kue, and he very strictly observes it : No Attribute that is Essential to God the Father (as Father) or Christ the Second Person in the Deity must come into his Creed, *i. e.* to be made a Necessary Article of it. And that the World may know that this is ac-

---

* De Uno Deo Patre. Sect. 1. cap. 1.

acceptable to the Party, one of them is chosen out to vindicate this Attempt of setting up One Article. A *Professed *Socinian* Writer (and no Alien, but true *English* Breed) undertakes it, and applauds the Author, and defends his Work: that it may publickly appear that this is the doctrine of the *Racovians* or *Anti-Trinitarians*, and that it was not only begun to be entertained by the *Ancient* and *Outlandish Socinians*, but that now, when it is fully improved, it is vouched by the *Modern* and *Native* ones.

But what may be the Reason why both the *Exotick* and *English Unitarians* agree to maim the Heads of Christianity, to contract its Articles, and to reduce it into so small a compass? Seeing there are *Several* Fundamental Truths appertaining to the Christian Religion, why are they not all pronounced Necessary to be believed and assented to? They have several reasons for this; first, they are compell'd to do it because otherwise they can't maintain that which so many of them profess to believe, *viz.* the Salvation of all men, of whasoever Per-

---

* The Exceptions of Mr. E. against the *Reasonableness of Christianity* examin'd.

Opinions Confuted. 65

Perſwaſion they are. This is an extravagant Principle which they have taken up, and it is the Modiſh Opinion at this day, but if they ſhould hold that there is a *Neceſſity* of believing a conſiderable number of Articles in Chriſtianity, they could not poſſibly entertain this Faſhionable Notion. Secondly, they cunningly keep up this Conceit of the neceſſity of but One Article, becauſe it makes for their own Preſervation and Safety, that neither the Magiſtrate nor Eccleſiaſtical Power in any Country may take occaſion to animadvert upon them : for why ſhould they trouble and moleſt them for holding ſuch doctrines as are not of the Foundation of Religion, as are of no Neceſſity to be believed ? This makes them forward to propagate their Notion. And hence alſo we ſee what is the reaſon of their talking ſo warmly for *Liberty :* This is done to Secure themſelves that though they broach never ſo Pernicious Opinions they may not fall under the laſh of the Magiſtrate. In brief, they would not be Puniſh'd here, and they think they have made ſure of hereafter by another Tenent of theirs. Thirdly, by vertue of this Expedient they can throw off any Doctrine when

F   they

they please, especially those Main Articles of the *Holy Trinity*, of *Christ's Satisfaction*, &c. for it is but saying that they are not necessary to be believed, (there being a Necessity of believing but One) and the business is done. Thus you see how it is their Concern to hold up their One Article.

But who sees not that hereby they deprefs Christianity, and unspeakably injure the Faith of the Gospel? What is the meaning of *Catechizing*, which hath been so universally commended and practised by the Ancients ? There were in the Primitive Church particular persons that made it their business to instruct and inform the ignorant in a *Catechetical* Way : yea, it was a Distinct Office among the Christians of old. Saint *Mark* in the Church of *Alexandria* was a *Catechist*, *Pantænus* succeeded him, then *Origen* had the same Employment there, and *Heraclius* after him. What ! was this only to teach *One Article* of Faith ? Who but a *Socinian* can believe this ? Is it not enough to rob us of our *God*, by denying *Christ* to be so, but must they spoil us of all the Other Articles of Christian Faith but One ? Who would think that the Popular Man ,
who

who pretends to take such care of the *Multitude,* should do them the greatest Mischief imaginable, whilest he makes a shew of being extraordinarily kind to them? for a greater Mischief there cannot be than to put them off with One Article of Christian Belief, when there are Many others of absolute necessity.

CHAP. V.

This Writer's doctrine tends to Irreligion *and* Atheism. *In what terms we may suppose the* Atheists *congratulate him. The clipping of the Articles of the* Creed *is a preparatory to the diminishing of the Precepts of the* Decalogue, *and the Petitions of the* Lord's Prayer. Obj. *Doth not the* frequent *mentioning of this Article* [Jesus is the Messias] *in the New Testament; yea, the* sole *mentioning of it in some places argue that there is no other Article of Faith which is necessarily to be believed but this?* Answ. *No: because* 1. *the believing of* Jesus *to be the promised* Messias *was the first step to Christianity, and therefore is so often propounded in the Evangelical Writings.* 2. *Though this* One *Article be mentioned alone in some places, it is to be supposed that* other *matters of Faith were at the same time proposed, though they are not recorded.* 3. *We must supply those places of Scripture where this* One *Article is set down alone from others which make mention of* Other Necessary Points of Belief. 4. *The clear discovery of the doctrines of the Gospel was* gradual; *and therefore we must not think that in the* Four Evangelists *and* Acts *are specified all the Necessary Articles of Faith, but we must look for some of them in the* Epistolary *Writings, when the Spirit of God had further enlightned the Apostles and other Christians.*

AND now, to prove yet further the *Pernicious* Nature of his Writings, doth any man doubt of their Tendency to *Irreligion* and *Atheism*? I charge him not with any such thing as a formal designing of this. (No: I will not entertain such a thought) but I only take notice how serviceable his Papers and Opinions are to this purpose. He hath mightily gratified the *Atheistical* Rabble by this his Enterprize, and accordingly we may suppose them in such Words as these to express their great Obligations and Thankfulness to him on this occasion; " We are beholding to this Worthy
" Adventurer for ridding the world of so
" Great an Encumbrance, *viz.* that
" huge Mass and unweildy Body of
" Christianity which took up so much
" room. Now we see that it was this
" *Bulk*, and not that of *Mankind* which he
" had an eye to when he so often menti-
" on'd

"on'd this latter. This is a Phyfician
"for our turn indeed: we like this Chy-
"mical Operator that doth not trouble
"us with a parcel of Heavy Drugs of no
"value, but contracts all into a Few Spi-
"rits, nay doth his bufinefs with a *Sin-*
"*gle Drop.* We have been in bondage a
"long time to *Creeds* and *Catechifms, Sy-*
"*ftems* and *Confeffions*, we have been
"plagued with a tedious Beadroll of *Ar-*
"*ticles* which our Reverend Divines
"have told us we muft make the matter
"of our *Faith.* Yea fo it is, both Con-
"formifts and Nonconformifts (though
"difagreeing in fome other things) have
"agreed in This to moleft and crucifie
"us. But this Noble Writer (we thank
"him) hath fet us free, and eas'd us by
"bringing down all the Chriftian Faith
"into One Point. We have heard fome
"men talk of the *Epiftolary* Compofures
"of the *New Teftament,* as if Great Mat-
"ters were contain'd in them, as if the
"great *Myfteries* of Chriftianity (as they
"call them) were unfolded there: but we
"could never make any thing of them;
"and now we find that this Writer is
"partly of our opinion. He tells us
"that thefe are Letters fent *upon occafion,*
"but we are not to look for our *Religi-*
"on

Opinions Confuted.

" *on (*for now for this Gentleman's sake we
" begin to talk of *Religion*) in these places.
" We believe it, and we believe that there
" is no Religion but in those very *Chap-*
" *ters* and *Verses* which he hath set down
" in his Treatise. What need we have any
" other part of the *New Testament?* That
" is Bible enough, if not too much.
" Happy, thrice happy shall this Au-
" thor be perpetually esteemed by us,
" we will Chronicle him as our Friend
" and Benefactor. It is not our way to
" *Saint* people: otherwise we would
" certainly *Canonize* this Gentleman,
" and, when our hand is in, his pair of
" Booksellers for their being so benefici-
" al to the World in Publishing so Rich a
" Treasure. It was a Blessed Day when
" this hopeful Birth saw the light, for
" hereby all the *Orthodox Creed-makers*
" and *Systematick Men* are ruined for ever.
" In brief, if we be for any *Christianity,*
" it shall be this Author's, for that
" agrees with us singularly well, it be-
" ing so short, all couch'd in four words,
" neither more nor less. It is a very
" fine Compendium, and we are infi-
" nitely obliged to this Great Reformer
" for it. We are glad at heart that *Chri-*
" *stianity* is brought so low by this Wor-
" thy

"thy Pen-man, for this is a good presage "that it will dwindle into Nothing. What! "but *One Article*, and that so *Brief* too! "We like such a Faith, and such a Re- "ligion because it is so near to None.

And is not the Reader satisfied that such language as this hath real Truth in it? Doth he not perceive that the discarding of all the Articles but One makes way for the casting off that too? And may we not expect that those who deal thus with the *Creed* will use the same method in reducing the *Ten Commandments* and the *Lord's Prayer*, abbreviating the former into One Precept, and the latter into One Petition? So that not only our Faith but our Practice and Devotion shall be crampt. There is as much reason to do one as the other: and they that have done the former will in time, it is no doubt, use the same discipline towards the latter, *i. e.* lop off some of the Precepts of the Decalogue, and diminish that Form and Pattern of Prayer which our Saviour hath left us.

Thus this Writer sees how fitly his book of the *Reasonableness of Christianity*, &c. *was brought into my Discourse about the Causes and Occasions of Atheism*, which he seems to wonder at, *p*. 2. It ap-

Opinions Confuted. 73

appears also that if *I gave his book an Ill Name* (as he complains,) it doth deserve it, and that it hath not only a *Socinian* but an *Atheistick Tang.* I have proved (and shall yet further do it in this present Undertaking) that he hath corrupted mens minds, depraved the Gospel, and abused Christianity. And is there no *Atheism* in this? To conclude, if after all he will stand to his Proposition, and assert there is but One Article of Faith (just one and no more, and it is sure there can be no less) necessarily to be assented to, he may enjoy his Confident Humour, but it is to be hoped that there is not any considerable number of men in the world that will admit of such an Unaccountable Paradox, and forfeit their Reasons merely to please their Fancy.

But because I design'd these Papers for the satisfying of the Readers *Doubts* about any thing occurring concerning the matter before us, and for the establishing of his wavering mind, I will here (before I pass to the Second General Head of my Discourse) answer a *Query* or *Objection* which some, and not without some shew of Ground, may be apt to start. How comes it to pass, they will say, that this

Article

Article of Faith, *viz.* that *Jesus is the Messias* or *Christ*, is so often repeated in the *New Testament*? Why is *this* sometimes urged without the mentioning of any *other* Article of Belief? Doth not this plainly shew that this is *All* that is requir'd to be believ'd as Necessary to make a man a Christian? May we not infer from the frequent and sole repetition of this Article in several places of the *Evangelist* and the *Acts* that there is no other Point of Faith of absolute necessity, but that this alone is sufficient to constitute a man a True Member of Christ?

To clear this *Objection*, and to give a full and satisfactory Answer to all doubts in this affair, I offer these ensuing Particulars, which will lead the Reader to the right understanding of the whole case.

1. It must be consider'd that the believing of *Jesus* to be the promised *Messias* was the *first step* to Christianity; and therefore This rather than any other Article was propounded to be believ'd by all those whom either our Saviour or the Apostles invited to imbrace Christianity. If they would not, if they did not give credit to This in the first place, viz. That *Jesus* of *Nazareth* was that
Eminent

Eminent and Extraordinary Perſon propheſied of long before, and that he was Sent and Commiſſion'd by God, there could be no hope that they would attend unto any other Propoſal relating to the *Chriſtian Religion.* This is the true reaſon why that Article was conſtantly propounded to be believ'd by all that look'd towards Chriſtianity, and why it is mention'd ſo often in the Evangelical Writings. It was that which *made way* for the embracing of all the other Articles, it was the *paſſage* to all the reſt. But our Anonymous Author not thinking of this, but obſerving that this One Article was uſually required to be aſſented to in the Goſpel-Writings, he thence inconſiderately concludes that this is the *Whole* of the Chriſtian Belief, and that there is nothing elſe to be *neceſſarily* aſſented to, to make a man a Chriſtian. I am ſorry to ſee that a perſon of ſome Senſe can have ſo little a feeling of the True Nature and Import of *Chriſtianity,* that he can harbour ſuch a thought as this, that all the neceſſary part of our Belief is ſumm'd up in a bare giving aſſent to this Propoſition, *Jeſus is the Meſſias.* He miſtakes a part of Chriſtian Faith for All, and the Entrance and Beginning
of

of it for the full Confummation of it.

2. It is to be remembred that though this One Propofition or Article be mention'd alone in fome places, yet there is reafon to think and be perfwaded that at the fame time *other* Matters of Faith were propofed. For it is confefs'd by all Intelligent and Obferving men that the Hiftory of the Scripture is concife, and that in relating of matter of Fact many paffages are omitted by the Sacred Penmen. Wherefore though but this One Article of belief (becaufe it is a Leading one, and makes way for the reft) be exprefly mention'd in fome of the *Gofpels*, yet we muft not conclude thence that no other matter of Faith was requir'd to be admitted of. For things are briefly fet down in the Evangelical Records, and we muft *fuppofe* many things which are not in direct terms related. The not attending to this hath been one occafion of the prefent miftake. Hence it was that this Narrow-minded Writer fhuts up all in the belief of *Jefus's* being the *Chrift*.

3. This alfo muft be thought of, that though there are Several parts and members of the Chriftian Faith, yet they do not all occur in any *One* place of Scripture.

ture. This is well known to thofe that are converfant in the Writings of the New Teftament, and therefore when in fome places only *One* fingle part of the Chriftian Faith is made mention of, as neceffarily to be imbrac'd in order to Salvation, we muft be careful not to take it alone, but to fupply it from feveral *other* places, which make mention of other Neceffary and Indifpenfable Points of Belief. I will give the Reader a plain Inftance of this, *Rom.* 10. 9. *If thou shalt believe in thy heart that God hath rais'd him* (i.e. the Lord Jefus) *from the dead, thou shalt be faved.* Here *One Article of Faith*, viz. the belief of Chrift's Refurrection (becaufe it is of fo great importance in Chriftianity) is only mention'd; but all the reft muft be fuppofed, becaufe they are mention'd in other places. And confequently, if we would give an impartial account of our Belief, we muft confult thofe places: and they are not all together, but difpers'd here and there : wherefore we muft look them out, and acquaint our felves with the Several Particulars which make up our Belief, and render it entire and confummate. But our hafty Author took another courfe, and thereby deceiv'd ceiv'd himself, and unhappily deceives others.

4. This (which is the Main Anfwer to the Objection) muſt be born in our minds that *Chriſtianity* was erected by degrees, according to that prediction and promiſe of our Saviour, that *the Spirit ſhould teach them all things*, John 14. 26. and that *he ſhould guide them into all truth*, John 16. 13. *viz.* after his Departure and Aſcenſion, when the Holy Ghoſt was to be ſent in a ſpecial manner to enlighten mens minds, and to diſcover to them the great Myſteries of Chriſtianity. This is to be Noted by us, as that which gives great light in the preſent caſe. The diſcovery of the Doctrines of the Goſpel was *Gradual.* It was by certain ſteps that *Chriſtianity* climb'd to its heighth. We are not to think then that all the Neceſſary doctrines of the Chriſtian Religion were clearly publiſh'd to the world in our Saviour's time. Not but that all that were neceſſary for *that time* were publiſhed: but ſome which were neceſſary for the *ſucceeding one* were not then diſcover'd, or at leaſt not fully. They had ordinarily no belief before Chriſt's *Death* and *Reſurrection* of thoſe Subſtantial Articles, *i.e.* that he
ſhould

should die and rise again : but we read in the *Acts* and in the *Epistles* that these were Formal Articles of Faith afterwards, and are ever since necessary to compleat the Christian Belief. So as to other Great Verities, the Gospel increased by degrees, and was not Perfect at once. Which furnishes us with a reason why most of the Choicest and Sublimest Truths of Christianity are to be met with in the *Epistles* of the Apostles, they being such doctrines as were not clearly discover'd and open'd in the *Gospels* and the *Acts*.

Thus I have, I conceive, amply satisfied the foregoing *Objection*, and I hope the Reader is convinc'd of the True Grounds why we must not expect all Necessary Points of Christianity in the Writings of the four Evangelists. If our present Writer had thought of this, and had distinguish'd of *Times*, he had not formed such an Ill Notion of *Christianity* as we find he hath done. But it is not only upon *Mistake* that this Author proceeds : his fault is much worse. It is too apparent that by this Abbreviating of *Christianity*, and by his voluntary neglecting what the *Epistolary* Writings deliver, he
de-

designs to exclude those Fundamental Doctrines which have been owned as such in the Church of Christ. So much for the *First General Head* which I propounded to insist upon.

CHAP.

CHAP. VI.

The next General Charge against him is, that the Texts of Scripture which respect the HOLY TRINITY are disregarded by him, or interpreted after the Anti-Trinitarian Mode. *This is proved from plain Instances. The latter more especially is evidenced from his interpreting the* Messias *and the* Son of God *to be the very same as to signification, and that no more is denoted by one term than by the other. The Weakness of the* Socinian *Arguing on this occasion fully laid open: and the Texts where these terms are mentioned plainly cleared. A Text produced and urged that confutes the vain surmises of the* Racovians *about those expressions, and that reduces them to an unavoidable* Absurdity. The Messias *is a Title of Chrift's Office:* The Son of God *is the Title of his Divinity. The former is founded on his Mission from the* Father: *The latter on his Peculiar Property as he is the Second Person in the Sacred Trinity; and consequently they are not synonymous terms. The Gentleman would wind in two Learned* Prelates, *but his attempt proves ineffectual.*

fectual. He is given to Shuffling. He abuses Scripture by quoting it.

MY *next Charge* against this Gentleman was this, that those Texts of Scripture which respect the Holy *Trinity* were either disregarded by him, or were interpreted by him after the *Antitrinitarian* Mode. And this he is so far from denying, that he openly avows it, *Vindic. p.* 22, 23. By which he hath made it clear that he espouses that doctrine of the *Socinians*. When I had offer'd those two plain Texts, *Mat.* 28. 19. *John* 1. 1. to prove the doctrine of the Blessed *Trinity*, he takes no care to give any Resolution about them, though he was absolutely oblig'd to do it, because those Texts are not in the *Epistles*, but in the *Gospels*, out of which latter he faith he made his *Collection of Articles*, but he should rather have said (and that with Truth) out of which he drew One Article. Nay, which is more strange, though he particularly mentions, *p.* 9. my taking notice of his omitting these Texts in his Treatise, nay though he sets them down at large in his *Vindication*, yet he hath the confidence to run presently to another thing, and

he

Opinions Confuted. 83

he shifts it off by one impertinent matter or other, and saith not one syllable with reference to those Famous Texts which are such remarkable testimonies to the doctrine of the *Trinity*. Who could do this but a *Socinianiz'd* Writer? And who could do this but a man that was wholly careless of his Credit, and did not care how he acted? And this very thing doth moreover shew that this Author (let him pretend what he will) is as great a despiser of the *Gospels* (when any thing in them doth not serve his turn) as he is of the *Epistles*. This will perpetually stick upon him, and he will never be able to wipe it off. If ever he accounts for this, he must at the same time make an acknowledgment of his crazy memory, and of something worse.

Again, as it is evident that he rejects the Doctrine of the Blessed *Trinity*, so more especially and particularly he waves that of the *Deity* of our Saviour. Which appears from this that he justifies the Charge against him, *viz.* that he made these terms [*the Messias*] and [*the Son of God*] the very same as to Signification, *p.* 23. *Vindic.* Which is the ve-

ry thing that * *Slichtingius* and other *Racovians* insist upon, and make a great stir about. And herein they write after †their Master, who largely pursues this Argument (for so he reckons it to be,) *viz.* that there is no difference between the Name *Christ* or *Messias* and that other *the Son of God.* He alledges the very same Text that our *Vindicator* doth, and some others. He argues from *Matt.* 16. 16. compared with *Luk.* 9. 20. *Thou art Christ the Son of the living God*, saith the former place: *Thou art the Christ of God*, saith the latter: therefore *Christ* and *the Son of God* are not only the same person, but these two expressions signifie the very same thing and no more. What a weak and pitiful Consequence is this? For it is grounded on this absurd bottom, namely, that when any of the *Evangelists* speak about the same matter, if one of them adds some words, yea, some material Passages which are not in the other, these must be reckoned to be the very same with what the other said, though they were utterly omitted by him. Then we may argue thus, St. *Matthew* saith, *Christ began to preach*,
and

---

* Cont. Meisner. de Trin. † Socin. cont. Wiek. cap. 5.

Opinions Confuted. 85

and to *say, Repent, Mat.* 4. 17. St. *Mark* faith, *He preach'd the Gospel, saying, Repent ye, and believe the Gospel, Mark* 1. 14, 15. therefore Repenting and Believing are the same, and there is no difference between them. Would not a Man be hooted at for such Arguing as this? Yet this is the very Reasoning of our *Racovian*, and of this late Proselyte of theirs. In one Evangelist he faith, our Saviour is called *Christ*, in another the *Son of God*, therefore the denominations of the *Son of God* and *Christ* are identified. Again, they endeavour to prove it from comparing *Mat.* 26.63. *Mark* 14. 61. with *Luk.* 22.67. In the former places 'tis related that the High Priest asked our Saviour whether he was *the Son of God, the Son of the Blessed:* in the latter, whether he was *the Christ*. Whence they roundly conclude that those Names *Christ and the Son of God* are synonymous. But they do this without any shew of reason, because they cannot (as * *Slichtingius himself* confesses) simply from an Omission infer the identity of the things which are expressed and which are left out, *viz* in the Writings

---

* Cont. Meisner. de Trin.

of the Evangelist: and consequently their Arguing is vain and groundless. The plain and satisfactory Answer to it is this, that St. *Luke* (guided by the Holy Ghost in giving the Narrative of what was done relating to our Lord) omitted the particular words which the other Evangelists have: and this is usual with all the Evangelists at one time or other. But a man can't infer thence that the words and expressions which are used by them are of the same import and signification. After this rate, when I read that *Christ fell upon his face*, *Mat.* 26.39. and that *he fell on the ground*, *Mark* 14.35. and that *he fell on his knees* for so 'tis in the Greek) *Luk.* 22.41. I may conclude that *face* and *ground* and *knees* are the very same thing, and one of them signifies no more than the other. This is the wild Logick of these men. Can there be a more extravagant way of talking than this? Especially if we remember what Pretences to Reason and Good Sense these men make above the rest of mankind. There are other Texts quoted by our Author to prove that there is no difference between *Christ* and *the Son of God* as to the signification of the words, but they may easily be answered from what

Opinions Confuted.

I have said concerning the interpretation of the foregoing Texts.

There is one place (to name no more) which confutes all the foresaid surmises of the *Socinians* about the identity of those Terms: it is that famous Confession of Faith which the *Ethiopian Eunuch* made when *Philip* told him that he might be baptized if he *believed*; *Acts* 8. 37. *I believe,* saith he, *that Jesus Christ is the Son of God.* This without doubt was said according to that apprehension which he had of *Christ* from *Philip*'s instructing him, for it is said *he preached unto him Jesus, v.* 35. He had acquainted him that Jesus was the *Christ*, the *Anointed* of God, and also that he was the *Son of God*, which includes in it that he was *God*. And accordingly this Noble Proselyte gives this account of his Faith, in order to his being baptiz'd, in order to his being admitted a Member of Christ's Church, *I believe that Jesus is the Son of God*, or you may read it according to the Greek, *I believe the Son of God to be Jesus Christ.* Where there are these two distinct Propositions, 1. That *Jesus* is the *Christ*, the *Messias*, 2. That he is not only the *Messias*, but the *Son of God*. If you do not own these two Propositions

ons included in his words, you muſt ſay that the *Eunuch* (though inſtructed by *Philip*) ſpoke Non-ſenſe, for if *to be Chriſt* and *to be the Son of God* are of the ſame ſignification, then his words ſound thus, *I believe that Jeſus Chriſt is Chriſt, I believe the Meſſias is the Meſſias*. This abſolutely follows from the foreſaid Notion, that *the Meſſias* and *the Son of God* are ſynonymous. So then here is an Abſurd Tautology inſtead of a Sober Confeſſion of Faith from this Eminent Convert: and *Philip* accepts of it as a good and right profeſſion of his Belief. This you muſt grant, or elſe you muſt acknowledg that the *Meſſias* and *Son of God* are not of the ſame ſignification, but are diſtinctly attributed to *Jeſus*. Theſe words will force you to acknowledg this, for in ſaying he believes *Chriſt to be the Son of God*, or that *the Son of God is Chriſt*, he lets us know that theſe two, *viz*. to be the *Meſſias* and to be the *Son of God* are different things (though they meet in the ſame Perſon) and conſequently that in all thoſe places (which are very many) where *the Son of God* is added to *the Meſſias*, we muſt underſtand it as an addition to the Senſe: whereas according to this Writer and his Complices theſe two are identified

Opinions Confuted.

tified: and consequently here is a *Nonsensical Reiteration* in the words, for they amount to no more than this, *I believe Jesus Christ to be Christ*. This is that Absurdity which they are reduced to.

But yet I will subjoyn this, that we are not unwilling to grant that our Saviour is sometimes call'd *the Son of God* because of his * Miraculous Conception, also because of the Dignity of his † Mission, and sometimes because of his ‖ Resurrection. But then we say that these do not exclude another, and higher cause of this Appellation, *viz.* his ** *Eternal Filiation:* he was begotten from Eternity of the substance of the Father by an ineffable Generation. If then we will speak of these two Denominations distinctly and properly, we must say that one is the Name of his *Office*, the other of his *Divinity*, and consequently that *Christ* and *the Son of God* are not expressions of the same latitude and import. And how indeed can they be? For they have different foundations, the one hath its rise from the Divine Mission, *viz.* that of the *Father*, who sent and anointed him

to

---

*Luke 1. 35. † John 10. 36. ‖ Acts 13. 32, 33.
** John 3. 16. Rom. 5. 8. 2 Cor. 11. 31.

to be a Saviour: the other is grounded in the fingular and peculiar Property of the Second Perfon in the Sacred Trinity, and fo is the Name of his Perfon. Wherefore it is moſt irrationally and abfurdly done of our Late Convert, in a fond Imitation of his Brethren, to confound thefe two which are really Diſtinct. I mention'd this as a proof of his being a *Socinian*, and he lets it remain a Proof, and fo do I. But here I would only obferve that he and they proceed in a *Prepoſterous* manner when they tell us that *Chriſt* is called *the Son of God*, becauſe of his Office and its Dignity, whereas it is evident that he had the Office and Dignity, becauſe he was *the Son of God*, and becauſe none could perform the Office but he that was fo. He was not *God* (a *Metaphorical God*, as the *Socinians* fometimes make him) becauſe he was *Chriſt* or the *Meſſias*: but he was the *Meſſias* becauſe he was *God*, even the *True God*. He was *the Chriſt of God* becauſe he was *the Son of God*: And this *Filiation*, in its ſtricteſt and propereſt fenſe, implies his *Divine Nature*, and his Coeſſentiality with the *Father*.

He would here wind in (*p.* 23.) the late Archbiſhop of *Canterbury*, as if he under-

understood the foregoing Terms as the *Socinians* do. But his words that are cited do not necessarily import any such thing, for *Nathanael* might own our Saviour to be the *Messias*, and call him *the Son of God*, and yet it doth not follow thence that the signification of both these Appellations is the same, or that the *Archbishop* thought so. And he would make use of the Authority of an Other *Prelate*, now living, of extraordinary Worth and Learning, who speaking only in a *general* way represents these two as the same thing, *viz.* that *Jesus is the Christ*, and that *Jesus is the Son of God*, because these expressions are applied to the same Person, and because they are both comprehended in one general Name, *viz. Jesus*. Yet it doth not follow thence but that if we will speak strictly and closely we must be forced to confess that they are of different significations; for we have different Ideas and notions of them, the one being the Name of our Saviour's Office, the other of his Person and Eternal Filiation. But our Gentleman adheres to his good Patrons and Friends the *Racovians*, and pronounces them the very same. And we may, for this as well as other reasons, pronounce
him

him the fame with thofe Gentlemen. Which you may perceive he is very apprehenfive of, and thinks that this will be reckon'd a good Evidence of his being what he denied himfelf to be before. *The Point is gain'd*, faith he, *and I am openly a Socinian.* p. 23. He never uttered truer words in his life, and they are the Confutation of all his Pretences to the contrary. This Truth, which unwarily dropt from his pen, confirms what I have laid to his charge, that he did read the forefaid Texts with *Socinian* Spectacles, that he interpreted them after the *Racovian* Mode, that he paffed by Other Texts, yea, the *Whole Epiftles* themfelves, becaufe he was fenfible how many Illuftrious Atteftations to the doctrine of the ever to be Adored Trinity are contained in them.

It is true, he tells us that *he never read the Socinian Writers*, p. 22. but we know his Shuffling is fuch that there is no depending on his word. But fuppofe he did not *read* thofe Authors, yet he doth not deny that he hath *Convers'd* with fome of them, and hath heard their Notions and Arguments: and this indeed he intimates to us when he lets us know that the *generality of Divines* he more converfes *verses with* are not *Racovians*, *p.* 22. which intimates that there are some *Particular Divines* he *less converses with* that are of another way. What shall we say? The Gentleman is a *Racovian*, and yet pretends he doth not know it. So we must number him among the *Ignoramus-Socinians* (as they tell us in their late Papers of *Ignoramus Trinitarians*) which is one sort of those folks it seems.

I will only further take notice here of what was truly said before he was aware, that *it was a dull work with him to quote Scripture, p.* 25. He hath sufficiently convinced the world, in his numerous Quotations of Scripture, that it was so. He might have added, it is *a diabolical work*, for in quoting Scripture after that rate which he is guilty of, he doth but follow his Pattern in *Mat.* 4. 6. His handling of Scripture, and making that use of it which he doth, is an Abusing of it. Such treating of the Holy Book is desecrating it; and whilest he talks Scripture, he prophanes it. So that *a Socinian begins to mend when he leaves this work off*, (*p.* 25.) in comparison of what he did before. So much for the Second Charge.

CHAP.

Some Late Socinian

CHAP. VII.

The last General Charge against him is, that when he professedly enumerates the ADVANTAGES of our Saviour's Coming, he hath not one syllable of his SATISFYING for us. *Hence it is rationally inferr'd that he favours* Racovianism. *He endeavours to evade this by pretending that in other places he uses such terms as import* Satisfaction. *Herein he is refuted. His* Dissimulation *discovered. Even whilest he proclaims himself a* Socinian, *he labours to disguise it. Which argues his* Weakness *and* Insincerity. *His Book is unworthy of the specious* Title *which he prefixes to it. The* Author's *Conclusion of the foregoing debates.*

ANother Proof, or rather Demonstration of our Author's being a Disciple of *Socinus* is this, that when he mentions the *Advantages and Benefits of Christ's Coming into the world*, he hath not one *syllable of his Satisfying for us, or by his Death purchasing life and salvation, or any thing that sounds like it.* He makes nothing of the force of this Evidence, wherefore it will be proper now to set it

be-

Opinions Confuted.

before the Reader in its true and native light. He that was giving an Account of the *Reasonableness of Christianity*, and was more particularly making it his *business* to shew for what *End* and *Purpose* Christ appear'd in the flesh, and to let his Readers know what *Good* and *Advantage* were brought to them by the *Messias*, he (I say) when he was about this work, and *Designedly* undertook it in this part of his book, was obliged to declare that one great Advantage of the *Messias*'s Coming was to take away our sins by Expiating them, that one Main End of his Coming was to make Satisfaction for us, and thereby to purchase life and glory. But this New Convert hath not any thing that sounds like it in this place, where he *professedly* took upon him to acquaint us *what are the Advantages* which accrue to us by the *Messias*. Though he hath the confidence to struggle with many other parts of the *Charges* against him, yet here he submits, and grants *(p.* 5. *Vind.)* he hath no such thing in the place where the *Advantages* of Christ's Coming are purposely treated of. And if by his own acknowledgment he hath no such thing when he reckons up the *Advantages* and *Blessings* of Christ's appearing in the world,

world, then every intelligent man knows what Inference to make, *viz.* that this Author was of opinion that Christ came not to Satisfie for us, and to purchase life for us by vertue of his Death, which is one of the Grand Points of *Socinianism*.

The force of this Inference is unavoidable, and it will attack our Adversary, be he never so cunning at Evasions, be he never so closely intrench'd in his Equivocations. For where should we expect this to be mention'd, if it be not expresly taken notice of in that part or division of his Treatise where he Purposely sets forth the *Benefits* of the Messias's Arrival? If he doth not make express mention of it here, it is either because he forgot it, (but he owns no such thing) or because he was careless (but he doth not think himself, whatever others do, to be such a Writer) or because he wilfully left it out, and this indeed is the true Reason: for all the world cannot but see (notwithstanding his Shifts) that his Subject engag'd him to reckon This in the number of the *Benefits* accruing by the Coming of Jesus Christ, if he had thought it to be one. When he was enumerating of those, this could not possibly have been omitted, because by all Writers that are not *Socinians*

nians this is always put into the Catalogue of those Blessings which we share in by the Undertakings of our Blessed Saviour. Hence it appears how impertinent and ridiculous that is, *It was not in the place he (* meaning *me) would have it in, p.* 5. He should have said, it is not in the place where every one might reasonably have look'd for it, it was not in the place where his matter necessarily oblig'd him to insert it, so that he was both faithless to his Subject, and false to the True Cause: in brief, it was not in that place where, if he had not been a Pupil of *Socinus*, it would certainly have been found: for no man but such a one did ever designedly undertake the Enumeration of those *Benefits* which we are partakers of by our Lord's Coming, and yet omit at the same time his Redeeming and Purchasing us by his Blood.

He pretends indeed, *p.* 5. that in another place of his book he mentions Christ's *restoring all mankind from the state of death,* and *restoring them to life,* and *his laying down his life for an other,* as our Saviour professes he did. These *few* words this *Vindicator* hath pick'd up in his book since he wrote it. This is *all* thro' his whole Treatise that he hath dropt concerning that Advantage of Christ's

Incarnation which I was speaking of: and they are general terms too, and such as every *Racovian* will subscribe to; for they are not backward to own that Christ some way or other (but not That before specified) *restored us to life*, and they cannot gainsay the express words of Christ concerning his *laying down his life for his sheep*, *John* 10. 15. but it is well known that (notwithstanding this) they deny the *Satisfaction* of Christ, and his purchasing life and salvation by vertue of his Meritorious Passion and Death. There is not any thing that *sounds* like this in that part of his Discourse where he peculiarly made it his employment and task to let the Reader know what Advantages we reap by our Saviours assuming our humane nature.

But he deridingly cries out *What will become of me, that I have not mention'd* SATISFACTION ? *p. 6*. I will tell you, Sir, (seeing you would know) what will become of you; you will ever hereafter be reckon'd by all understanding men an Egregious Whiffler, or in plain terms a Notorious Dissembler. For the case stands thus, (and I doubt not but the Reader will perfectly agree with me in it) you believe Christ's *Satisfaction*, or you do not: if you believe there is
such

Opinions Confuted. 99

such a thing, and this was one of the *Advantages* we have by Christ's Coming, then you were false and treacherous in omitting it: if you believe it not, you are as false and hypocritical in vouching your self to be no *Socinian*, seeing this is one known Badg of a person of that Character.

Let him take which of these ways he will, he forfeits his Truth and Integrity. Was it not enough to make use of the Chief *Socinian* Arguments, and to expound Texts in the *Racovian way*, and to leave out plain and direct places even in the very *Gospels* that assert the Holy *Trinity*, and moreover to throw off all the Famous Testimonies to this doctrine in the *Apostolical Epistles*, and to balk the *Satisfaction* of Christ for us, even when he was purposely telling the Reader what are the *Advantages* which flow to us from Christ's Coming? Was it not enough, I say, to do all this (which loudly proclaims him a *Socinian*) but must he also hold the world in hand that he is none? Can this Writer himself consider this, and not blush? Who doth not wonder at his *Weakness*, that he should manifestly take the part of these Gentlemen and yet endeavour to perswade us that he is not of their number? But who doth not wonder more at his *Insincerity*, that he should

should act thus? Must not this then be his Lasting Character that he hath in his Writings demonstated himself to be not only a *Socinian*, but a *False hearted* one?

There are other Passages in his book which I might produce to confirm this Character of him, but those may be taken notice of at another time. At present let it suffice that I have shew'd that he hath not said one word in his *Vindication* that clears him of this imputation. And as for his book it self of the *Reasonableness of Christianity*, let it suffice to say that though there have been many Treatises concerning that Subject, yet none ever could imagine that this which he offers could possibly be brought under that *Title*. He saith some body is good at Conjecturing, but if a man had the best faculty in the world that way, it were impossible to guess and surmise that such a Title should be prefix'd those Papers which are an Unreasonable and False Representation of Christianity, a Lame and Shatter'd Account of the Principles of the Gospel, and, in short, a kind of Libel against the New Testament. Finally, let it suffice that I have demonstrated to the Reader that this Gentleman acts a Part in what he writes; by which

he

Opinions Confuted. 101

he hath gained this, that he muſt never be believed for the future. He that is ſuch an Under-hand dealer can't be truſted: there is no heed to be given to what he ſaith.

Thus I thought my ſelf obliged to ſet before the Reader the ſtate of the Caſe between this Gentleman and my ſelf, and to give an impartial account of our Sentiments. I am ſatisfied in my Undertaking, for (whatever my defects in it otherwiſe be) I'm ſure I have aimed aright, at the vindicating the Glory of the Great Majeſty of heaven and earth. I have faithfully aſſerted our Holy Religion, and the Divinity of the Bleſſed Author and Founder of it. I have maintained the Authority and Honour of the Holy Scriptures. To the purſuing of which Glorious Deſigns I ſhall dedicate my whole life: and I hope from what I have written, and ſhall hereafter write, the World will bear me witneſs that I do ſo.

CHAP. VIII.

The Gentleman inſinuates that the Author *would repreſent every one as an* Atheiſt *that thinks not as he doth. This Calumny is baffled. He laughs at* Orthodoxy, *and cries down* Syſtems *and* Creeds. *This Indifferent Writer blames the* Author

thor *for his* Zeal. *Is angry with him for penetrating into his Thoughts and Intentions. The Party inure themselves to* Sophistry, *and yet make a shew of Simplicity and Plainness. The Gentleman's Uneven Temper observ'd. What is meant by* a known Writer of the brotherhood. *He is himself of an other* Fraternity. *Though he pretends to be Grave, he Scoffs and Jeers. He cannot be brought to confess himself to be a Retainer to* Socinianism, *though he hath given such evident proofs of his being one. The Author shuts up all with seasonable Advice to him, giving him some account of the* Freedom *which he hath used towards him in the preceding Discourse.*

Having now dispatch'd my Main Business, and found the Bill against the Criminal, not by *Innuendo's* but by Plain Express Proof, I am at leisure to account with him for some Other Passages in his *Vindication*. He insinuates that I would represent every one as an *Atheist*, or a *Promoter of Atheism* that doth not think as I do, *doth not just say after me*, *p.* 1, 2. Which is a groundless Calumny, and might be confuted from that *Freedom* which I professed, *p.* 77. even

in

in that *Discourse* which he excepts against. I have always been averse to *Bigotism*, I never shew'd my self a Dogmatizer, but always declar'd for an Ingenuous Liberty, such as doth not audaciously encroach upon the Necessary and Fundamental Points of our Religion. Therefore this *Vindicator*'s wilful mistaking of what I said, thereby to represent me as extremely Censorious and Uncharitable, looks like Spleen. But I need say no more than this, that the Reader is convinc'd (I question not) from what hath been premised that this Writer will say any thing that comes into his head. This seems to be natural to him every where: and he can be no more without it than a Spaniard without his Guittar.

To be *Orthodox* is a great Scandal, it seems, and he often objects it to me: which, as the Learned know, was the very language and idiom of the *Arrians* of old, and of that sort of men who are since known by the name of *Socinians*. He speaks in the very Stile of the *Old Antitrinitarians*; though it may be he will say he doth not know it. He publickly prides himself in his *Heterodoxy*, and hates even with a deadly hatred all *Catechisms* and *Confessions*, all *Systems* and *Models*,

dels, *p.* 8. He laughs at *Orthodoxy*, *p.* 17, 20. and derides *Mysteries*, which are infallible marks of a *Racovian* Brother. And O how he grins at the *Spirit of Creed-making* ? *p.* 18. *Vindic.* the very thoughts of which do so haunt him, so plague and torment him that he cannot rest till it be conjured down. And here, by the way, seeing I have mention'd his rancour against *Systematick books and writings*, I might represent the *Misery* that is coming upon all *Booksellers* if this Gentleman and his Correspondents go on successfully. Here is an effectual Plot to undermine *Stationers Hall*; for all *Systems* and *Bodies* of Divinity, Philosophy, *&c.* must be cashier'd: whatever looks like *System* must not be bought or sold. This will fall heavy on the Gentlemen of St. *Paul's Church-yard*, and other places.

This Author often finds fault with me for my *Zeal*, *p.* 5, 18, 37. It is likely he hath heard that when the Gospel was heretofore read in the Churches in *Poland* (before it was *Socinianized*,) it was usual to draw their Swords, to shew that they would defend it against all that opposed it. I do but draw my Pen in defence of the *Gospel*, yea and the *Epistles*, and I am censur'd as a *Zealot* by him.

And

Opinions Confuted.

And it is not ſtrange, for he muſt needs declare againſt *Zeal* that is *Indifferent.* Beſides, according to this Judicious Caſuiſt there is but *One* Point of Chriſtianity that a man can be zealous for, if he would. Queen *Mary*'s Martyrs fooliſhly threw away their lives, for neither *Bonner* nor any of their Perſecutors did ſo much as deſire them to renounce this Article *Jeſus is the Meſſias:* and as for all the reſt, this Gentleman tells us that they are *not neceſſarily to be believ'd,* and conſequently not to be acknowledg'd and profeſs'd; and then who will ſhew any *Zeal* for them, eſpecially ſuch as will carry a man into the Flames?

He often talks of *my being in his boſom, and knowing his heart and thoughts, p.* 14, 15, 24. (which by the by is more than his Brethren will allow *God himſelf* to know, for *Free Acts being uncertain they can't be certainly underſtood by God* (as the Gentleman whom I ſhall ſpeak a word with anon tells us.) This ſort of Talk argues that he is much troubled that I have penetrated into his *Thoughts,* and have diſcovered to the world what his Intention and Deſign is. And yet he intimates alſo by this way of ſpeaking that it is an Impoſſible thing to do this. How im-

impossible then is it for himself *to know his heart?* for this is a certain Maxim, It is the Punishment of a Dissembler to deceive himself, for his endeavouring to do so to others. I wish this Writer would consider of it, and learn for the future to be free, open and fair, and then others (as well as himself) would have a window into his breast, and see that which they are sorry they find no appearance of now.

And I wish this were not too common a fault of the Party, at least of many of them. They inure themselves to Sophistry, Cunning, and Artifice, when they either interpret Texts, or Argue in favour of their Darling Opinions. They then too palpably impose upon other mens minds, as well as upon their own. And yet at the same time they pretend to great Simplicity and honest dealing. Thus you find them applauding themselves in their late Prints: * *the Unitarians* (say they of themselves) *are plain fellows, and have Countrey Consciences, and do not like juggling.* You Gentlemen of the *City*, look to it: these *Unitarians*, these *Socinians* have a very bad opinion of you, for here they would have it believ'd that *City-Consciences* are false and per-

---
* The Trinitarian Scheme of Religion, *page* 21.

Opinions Confuted. 107

perfidious, deceitful and juggling. It is a courſe Complement, and Ruſtick enough which theſe *Plain Fellows* put upon you. It is not the firſt time they have ſtruck at you: *London* muſt be diſciplin'd by *Racovia*. And the *Vindicator* is one of theſe *Plain Fellows*, for as he hath ſhew'd himſelf an *Unitarian*, ſo he makes it appear that he hath a *Country-Conſcience* in the ſenſe that theſe men ultimately mean it in, *viz.* a knack of Cheating in a Ruſtical plain way, as when he pretends to make a Religion for the *Rabble*, an *Eaſie Plain Religion*, a *Creed with One Article*, and no more; pretending thereby to gratifie *them*, but under hand ſubverting *Chriſtianity*.

Nor have I yet done with him. I find him to be a Man of a very Uneven Temper: ſometimes he is very Low and Whining, and will be *asking pardon*, and *deſiring me*, &c at other times he is Imperious and Magiſterial, and *requires me*, &c. Sometimes he talks very demurely, as about being *in earneſt*, *p. 9. being ſerious and grave*, *p. 24, 25.* and in a Pedantick Humour he undertakes to cenſure and correct my *Stile*, *p. 24.* But this fit of Gravity doth not laſt long; he every where ſhews himſelf Light and Freakiſh,

Iro-

Ironical and Abusive as far as he is able, and nibbles at Wit according to his mean Talent. He inveighs forsooth against *Declamatory Rhetorick, Wit and Jest,* &c. *p.* 24. *Vindic.* and yet at the same time is Wanton and Frolick, Starting any thing to sport himself with. In that very place before mention'd where he seems to put on his Gravity, he hath not forgot *the Merry time of Rope-dancing and Puppet-Plays,* at which he was good in the days of yore. It is likely he had been a little before conducting some of his Young Brood to *Bartholomew Fair,* and thence this precious idea came into his head.

Without doubt he thought he was not a little Ingenious in that waggish expression, *p.* 6. *a Known Writer of the brotherhood:* which is meant of the Brethren of the Clergy who have writ against the *Socinian* Cause, the same with the *Popular Authorities* and *Frightful Names* which he speaks of, *p.* 23. The professed Divines of *England* you must know are but a pitiful sort of folks with this great *Racovian Rabbi.* He tells us plainly that he is not mindful of what *the Generality of Divines declare for, p.* 22. He labours so concernedly to engratiate himself with the *Mob,* the *Multitude* (which he so often

ten talks of) that he hath no regard to these. *The generality of the Rabble* are more considerable with him than *the generality of Divines, the Writers of the brotherhood.* Though truly a Wise Man that hears any one judg thus, will think he deserves as well to be rewarded with a pair of Ears of the largest size as *he* did who judg'd on *Pan*'s side against *Apollo*. But there is more yet in this term of *brotherhood* than this, for here it is implied (and his thoughts may be suppos'd to be upon it when he wrote) that he himself is a Writer of an *Other Fraternity*; and truly this Stile is very proper, for the men of that Party (as 'tis well known) have labour'd to signalize themselves (in the Writings that they have publish'd) by the Title of *Brethren*. It is agreed then; we will for the future take him for a *Polonian Brother*. And I ask the Reader whether this *Brother* be not of kin to the Order of *Friers* in *Italy* who were call'd *Fratres Ignorantiæ, viz.* because, they professed to teach the people as little as possibly they could, as suppose *One Article of Religion*, and no more.

I might proceed further, and shew that this Author, as Demure and Grave as he would sometimes seem to be, can

scoff

scoff at the Matters of Faith contain'd in the Apostles *Epistles*, *p.* 18. *l.* 4. *&c.* To coakse the *Mob* he prophanely brings in that place of Scripture, *Have any of the Rulers believ'd in him?* *p.* 33. Ridiculously and Irreligiously he pretends that *I prefer what he saith to me to what is offer'd to me from the Word of God,p.*25. What is there that this Gentleman will not turn into Ridicule or Falsity? What is there that he will not take hold of to be Sportive and Gamesome? We may further see how Counterfeit his *Gravity* is whilst he condemns *frothy and light discourses*, *p.*26.*Vindic.*and yet in many pages together most irreverently treats a great part of the *Apostolical Writings*, and throws aside the Main Articles of Religion as unnecessary. From all which it is clear that he contradicts and opposes himself. Whence by the by we may gather that when he saith he is *no Socinian*, we must take his meaning to be that *he is one*, for he is made up of Contradictions. I observed before that the *Dissenting Ministers confess'd to him* (if you will believe * him) *that they understood not the difference in debate among them:* but this Gentleman can't be brought to *confess* any thing, he
will

---
* Reasonableness of Christianity, *p.* 303.

will not own that he is *a Writer of the brotherhood*. No: there is some great Reason (if it may be call'd so) for this, that he would not be thought to be of *Sozzo*'s side: though the Marks and Tokens are so plain that he may be apprehended without a Hue and Crie.

Come, Good Sir, do not act a part any longer: They have been desirous to put you upon service, and you were as willing to be employ'd in it: but now at last Confess it. Appear no more in Masquerade: away with this Mummery, and shew your self what you are. You have let the world see (and so far we are beholding to you) that *Socinian* is a Reproachful Title; that any one may gather from your being so backward to own it. You would never have taken so much pains to shift off this Character if it were not a very Scandalous One. Throw off your Vizour then, and speak out like a Man. Be free and ingenuous, and dissemble not with Heaven as well as Men. I have, Sir, been very free with you, which you may impute to your not being so with your self. You know the Rule among the Men of Art, The Heart is known by the Pulse. I have made bold to usurp upon the Faculty, I have been

feel-

feeling your Pulse, and I have found that it strongly beats after the *Racovian* tone. This I have told you with some plainess, and you are obliged to me for representing you to your self. I know you did not expect an Assault, for it was your self (however you apply it to me) that was thought to be one of * *the most Priviledged sort of men*. But, Sir, in the Reign of Truth *Protections* are not of any use. It is a laudable way sometimes to fight the Enemy in his Trenches. There are some Criminals that must be snatch'd from the horns of the Altar, especially when they injure the Altar it self, when they abuse that which is Holy, and trample upon our Sacred Faith and Religion.

To conclude, I have said nothing out of prejudice or disgust, much less out of bitterness and ill will, for I am in Entire Charity with you, and the more so because I have spoken so freely. If you complain now (as you did before) that you are *hardly dealt with*, I have only this to say, A Plain Down-right Adversary might perhaps have met with another usage, but such a Stubborn Dissembler could not expect *fairer quarter*.

A

---

* Vindic *p*. 20.

A
Brief REPLY
To Another
SOCINIAN Writer,

Whose Cavils bear this Title,

[The Exceptions of Mr. *Edwards* in his *Causes of Atheism* against the *Reasonableness of Christianity*, &c. Examin'd.]

A

Brief REPLY

To another

SOCINIAN Author.

THERE came lately to my hand this Writer's Sheets in the true *Racovian Print*: but I having been so large upon the *Vindicator*, this *Double-Column'd* Gentleman, who pretends to be an *Examinator*, cannot expect I should spend much time about him. In the first place we are to observe that he most humbly and reverentially *dedicates* his Papers to the New Patron of the Cause, and takes upon him the Defence of what he hath said in his *Reasonableness of Christianity*. He highly applauds him for his being so serviceable to the *Socinian* and *Antitrinitarian* Interest. And it is part of his Panegyrick that *he hath happily provided for the quiet and satisfaction of the minds of the honest multitude, p.* 3. That is, he hath not troubled and molested them (as some have done with propounding Several Articles of Christian Belief) but hath told them that *One* is enough for them, and bids them rest contented with that, like good honest Ignorant Souls. Thus *he hath provided* (but how *happily* let the Reader judg) *for their quiet and satisfaction.* But though the *Examinator* heaps great Commendations on the *Vindicator*, yet he professes if (you'll believe him, you may) that *he knows him not, p* 4. Only at a venture he takes his part, he now being become one of the *Brotherhood,* and may prove a very Substantial Tool and Engine in the great Work they are now about, *viz.* the subverting of our Saviour's *Divinity*, the laying aside the *Apostolical Epistles*, the shutting out the *Necessary Matters of Faith* contain'd in them, and the setting up and idolizing of *One Article*, with defiance of all the rest as any ways Necessary to be believ'd. This is the New *DIANA* that is set up by our *Ephesians,* especially by their late *Demetrius.*

Then he hath a fling at my *Booksellers, p.* 5. wherein he follows the steps of the *Vindicator, p.* 37. And in this and other things

Opinions Confuted. 117

things they jump, which discovers their Correspondence, though he had but just before said *he knew him not*. And so this gives us an account of the truth of what the *Vindicator* said, that *he knew not that the Socinians interpreted such and such Texts after such a manner*. This is said to impose upon the world, and make them believe that he and the *Racovians* have not been Confederates. But he confutes this in another place, where he owns that he hath particular knowledg of that Gentleman, and knew the circumstances of his Life, *p.* 13. *Col.* 2. for he could not say of him that *he overcame the prejudices of Education* unless he had been acquainted with his Education and manner of life. And if this is *the Gentleman of no ordinary judgment*, from whom he saith *he hath seen a Letter*, &c. *p.* 17. Here still you see is Juggling and sleight of hand, and it is natural and proper it seems to the Party. And further to shew their Conferring of Notes together, it might be observ'd that both agree to say that what I write was writ in *haste* and in a *fit*, *Examin. p.* 5. *Vindicat. p.* 19. And let it be so, if they will, for thence it will appear that a man need not take up much time to confute either the *Vindicator* or this Gentleman.

I 3   But

But what is this that he hath to say of my *Bookſellers?* Some great matter without doubt. *He put me upon making Exceptions againſt that Treatiſe, that ſo the ſale of his own Tract might be the more promoted,* p. 5. The Reader may gueſs from this what is their own Trade; they and their Bookſellers joyntly club to cheat the poor bulk of mankind. That is their practice we may learn from their faſtning it upon others. Any man may ſee that the *Rationaliſt* went ſnips with his *Pater-Noſter-Men*, they fully underſtood one another, as appears from their not denying him to be the Author of the *Reaſonableneſs of Chriſtianity*, &c. all the time it was in the Preſs: but when they ſaw the Sale of it was not according to their High Expectations, they, to buoy up the Gentleman's Credit, began to diſown him to be the Author This was done by the two *Shrinemen* that before cried aloud for *Diana.* Now then, I think it appears at laſt that theſe people are extremely beholding to *my Bookſellers* if they did any ſuch thing as they ſurmiſe, for by this means the ſale of *their Book* was promoted.

After the *Bookſellers,* I muſt be taken to task by the Reverend *Examinator,* who
having

having flutter'd a little about the *formal words* which I had said were to be found in *the Reasonableness of Christianity* (which no Creature that hath once read it will once doubt of) he fixes on this (*p.* 5.) as the *Vindicator*'s true sense, yea his own words, *that all that was to be believed for justification, or to make a man a Christian, by him that did already believe in, and worship one True God, maker of heaven and earth, was no more than this Single Proposition, that Jesus of Nazareth was the Christ or the Messias.* This man makes a Miserable Entrance to his work, for though he saith these are the Vindicator's words (for thus he brings them in, *It is true he faith*) yet no man alive can find them in his book: and he knew this himself, else he would have set down the page, as we find him paging it afterwards. What shall we say then to such men as these who will vouch any thing? They can be trusted with no book, no not with one of their own Tribe, for we see here that this Writer's stile is, *he saith,* and yet this Express *Saying* no where occurs in the book he refers to. And here by the way, we may observe the bold Partiality of this Writer; he (as well as the *Vindicator*, *p.* 38.) would charge me with not quoting the *formal words* which are in the *Reasonableness of Christianity*, whilest he is not sensible of his plain misquoting the same Author. Yet here we may observe this, that it is but a *Single Proposition* (and no more) which is to be believ'd, to make a man a Christian. This is the sense of the *Vindicator*'s friend, thus he understands him; and so indeed every one must, and yet it may be remembred that the Vindicator himself would evade this, and pretends that he means more than a Single Proposition or Article.

Now next let us see how this *Examinator* licks over the *Vindicator*'s Article, and tells us that the belief of *Jesus*'s being the *Messias comprehends* and *implies several other things, p.3.* Here he sweats to bring off his Brother handsomly and with credit by letting us know that his Bold Assertion which runs through his whole book is to be *qualified* after this manner, 1. *All synonymous expressions*, &c. and so he sets them down one, two and three. But I ask him this Question (and let the Reader be pleas'd to observe the issue of it) Why did not the Gentleman himself make use of these *Qualifications* when he vented the Proposition, and insisted upon it in

the

Opinions Confuted.

the bulk of his book, yea why did he not mention these *Qualifications* in his *Answer* to any Exceptions against his book? He knew what he had asserted, and he defends (as well he can) his doing so, but you will find in no part of his *Vindication* that he betakes himself to these *Evasions*, though he hath enough of Others of a different sort. How then come you, Mr. *Examinator*, to invent these things for him? Do you not hereby proclaim to the world that you will put off the Reader with any idle and groundless Conceit of your own?

When he repeats my words, *p.* 6, 7. wherein I took notice of the Gentleman's *willful omitting of plain and obvious passages in the Evangelists* (out of whose Writings he had drawn a Whole Article) *which contain the belief of the Holy Trinity*, he saith not a word to excuse his *Omission*, but by his silence (for he would have spoken without doubt if he had had any thing to say in his Friends defence) he owns it to be wilful and blameable. Only he comes with the Trite and Common Answer of the Party to those Texts; but before he enters upon the Second of them, *viz. John* 1. 1. he declares *there is no such Text in the whole Bible, p.* 9. He

said

said rightly that *he was bold to say it,* for a man shall scarcely hear a more Audacious word, though 'tis true he endeavours to mollifie it with an *if.*

As to what he saith about my taking notice of the Gentleman's slighting the *Epistolary Writings,* I have fully answered it in the foregoing Papers, and therefore shall add no more here.

He proceeds next to those *Socinan Authors,* whose undue Notions concerning God I glanc'd upon. The Author of *the Considerations,* &c. in reply to the Right Reverend Bishop who had from the notion of *God's Eternity* inferr'd that he was *Self-existent* or *from himself,* hath these words, *What makes him (viz.* the Bishop) *say, God must be from himself, or self-originated? for then he must be before he was,* which this Writer concludes to be a Contradiction. Therefore he would make this Conclusion that God's *Self-existence* is a Contradiction. I know it will be pretended that this is the Consequence only of the Bishops Notion of *Eternity,* but it is plain that that Writer makes use of this Arguing to shake the belief of the *Eternity* and *Self-Existence* of the Allmighty, and that will appear from what he further adds in way of Exception to what that Reve-

Opinions Confuted. 123

Reverend Person saith afterwards concerning God's Eternity. This *Examinator* talks of a *false notion of Self-existence,* but doth not say what it is. If I have mistaken the *Considerer,* let him write plainer another time.

As to the *Examinator*'s question, How the *Second* and *Third Persons* can be *Self-existent?* I answer, They are Self-existent as they are eternally from the Self-same Deity. Though according to the *Nicene* Creed Christ be *God of God,* yet that doth not infring his *Self-Existence,* because those words are not spoken of the *Essence* of Christ which is common to him with his *Father,* but of his *Personality.* He being the same with the *Father* as to the former hath his Existence of himself; but differing from the *Father* as to the latter, he is rightly said to be *from him,* or *of him* as he is the Second Person in the Trinity. This is easily reconciled with what he saith an Other Bishop asserts, if this *Unitarian* hath not a mind to quarrel.

In the next Paragraph he is quite non-plus'd, for I had charg'd the *Socinian* Authors with their denial of *God's foreknowing future Contingencies,* and consequently denying the *Omniscience* of God, which
is

is an inseparable Attribute of the Deity; and he having nothing to reply to the purpose, first tells us *he is not concern'd in it*, *p.* 18, whereas every one knows that he being one of the Party is concern'd. Secondly, assoon as he had as it were renounced the *Socinian* doctrine by saying he was not Concern'd in it, he presently owns it for Truth, as those words import, *p.* 18.-- *to deny his foreknowledg of the certainty of that which is not certain*,&c. which is as much as to say that there are some things that are Uncertain and therefore Unknowable and these God can have no knowledg of. And yet thirdly, he would seem to hint that *it is a dishonourable thing to God* (those are his words) that he should not have a foresight of these things. Thus Confused is our Author, which shews he is not fit to be an *Examiner* of other mens Writings, when he can't write Consistently himself, but in three or four lines hath as many Blunders.

In the next words and what follows he perfectly gives up the Cause, *p.* 18. for I had laid this to the charge of the *Racovians* that they denied the *Immensity* or *Omnipresence* of God, which is a Property or Perfection never to be disjoyn'd from

Opinions Confuted. 125

from the Deity; whereupon he tamely acknowledges that *Crellius* and the rest of the Fraternity are of this perswasion. Only, because the Gentleman must be wagging his tongue, he gives us a scrap out of a *Latin Poet*, and just names a *Greek Father*, who never said any thing to that matter, and so we are rid of them.

But he comes on again, and goes off assoon, for he barely mentions the *Spirituality* of God, which I had asserted to be another Divine Excellency: and it is such an Attribute of God that we can't conceive of him without it, and therefore it is made the short and comprehensive Definition of him that *he is a Spirit*, *John* 4. 24. In my Discourse which this *Examinator* calls in question I took notice that the *Socinians* denied this Property of the Deity, which I justly tax'd as an *Atheistick Tang*: and I think it was a mild term, for it is a Rank Sign of a great tendency to Atheism to deny that God is a *Spirit*, *i. e.* an Immaterial Incorporeal Being. But our present Author resolves himself into the opinion of those *modest Divines* (who by their Blushing can be no other than *Socinus*'s Scholars) who determine nothing about the Point; which is as much as to say, he and they
de-

deny it. But you must know they are now a little upon their Credit: this Gentleman (who speaks in the name of the rest) had before given up the *Immensity* and *Omniscience* of God, and therefore it is high time now to be upon the Reserve, and to pause a little, that the world may not see that they reject All those Properties of the Deity which I mention'd. But notwithstanding this cunning practice of theirs, the world may see, yea, it cannot but plainly see that they deny every one of these Divine Attributes more or less, and this particularly which I mention'd last, *viz.* that *God is a Spirit* properly so call'd. For whereas I quoted *Socinus* and *Crellius* (their Grand Patriots) to prove this denial, this Writer takes no notice of my doing so, which lets us see that the opinion of those Great Masters is humbly submitted to by all the rest.

So now I hope the Reader is convinc'd that I was not *Unjust* to the *Socinians*, that I did not *highly injure* them (as they have cried out) when I charg'd them with *Atheism* or a *Strong Tendency* to it in some Points. I tax'd them with denying these four Attributes, the *Self-Existence*, the *Omniscience*, the *Omnipotence*, the

Opinions Confuted. 127

the *Spirituality of God*, and lo! this professed Son of *Socinus* (who was chosen out with great deliberation and judgment without doubt from the rest of his brethren to undertake the Cause, to refute what I had alledg'd against them, and who questionless hath said all that he could in the Case) lo! I say, this professed and *known Writer of the Brotherhood* confirms and ratifies what I have laid to their charge. For he produces the words out of their own Author which I referr'd to, whence it appears that he had a mind to distort the Right Reverend Bishop of *Worcester*'s words, and to argue against the *Self-Existence* of God. This *Examinator* without any more ado rejects the Second and third Attributes, and by his boggling at the fourth we know what must be the fate of that. Thus he and his fellow-Criminals being conscious to the truth and Justice of the Charge, confess themselves *Guilty*. They are so far from clearing themselves of the Imputation and Enditement that they Aggravate it. I leave the Reader to give the *Sentence*. They deserve a Severe one at his hands, but I desire him to be Merciful for the sake of our Lord JESUS CHRIST, who forgave and pray'd for

his

his greatest Opposers. May the All-Merciful God forgive them, and enlighten their minds, that they may be convinc'd of their Errors, and heartily renounce them. The Lord *give them Repentance to the acknowledging of the truth, that they may recover themselves out of the snare of the devil.*

Then he runs to their *Common Place*, which hath help'd to fill up their papers many a time, and he thinks he doth great feats. But he only epitomizes *Crellius de Uno Deo Patre*, and offers a great many Texts *which have been answered a hundred times*, as he (but untruly) saith on another occasion, *p.* 8. This takes up 18 or 19 whole Pages: and why? Because this costs him nothing, he borrows it all (and he might have borrow'd a great deal more) from the same Author. Here he can afford to be very long and large, but when he undertakes the *Examination* of what I had *particularly objected* against the *Socinians*, he is like the dog at *Nilus*, he is presently gone: he is not furnish'd with any Answer that he dares insist upon, or trust to.

Next, I will observe to the Reader that this Author meddles not with my *Argument* which I drew from their own

Profeſſed Principle, viz. that *nothing is to be believed but what is exactly adjuſted to Reaſon,* and thence prov'd that upon the ſame account that they reject the doctrine of the Holy *Trinity* they may likewiſe quit the belief of a *Deity.* This I enlarg'd upon in ſeven pages together, it being (as I then conceiv'd, and am more confirm'd in it ſince) an Unanſwerable Proof of what I laid to their Charge. He only grazes on it a little, *p.* 19. but wheels off preſently, and fixes upon that ſubject before mentioned, *God's Unity,* becauſe he knew where to have enough of it, but did not know how to take off the force of that *Argument* which I propounded and inſiſted upon.

In the next place he will turn *Critick,* and ſee whether he can thrive in this employment, ſeeing he hath ſo ill ſucceſs in his former attempts. His nice palate diſguſts the word *birth,* as applyed to *Adam, p.* 38. but thereby he only ſhews his want of skill in the Denotation of words. He is ſo poor a Dabbler in *Grammer* and *Criticiſm* that he knows not that by the Hebrew *jalad,* and the Greek γίνες and γιννᾶς, and the Latin *naſci,* and accordingly our Engliſh [*to be born*] are

ſig-

signified in a *general* way the *Origin, Rise,* or *Beginning* of things or persons, and consequently *Birth* or *Nativity* is not to be taken always in the Vulgar Sense. He might have read in *Genethliack* Writers that the word is applied even to *Cities* and *Houses*. But I need not go so far to defend the Expression. The use of it, and that in the very way that I have applied it, is to be found in Scripture: *Art thou the first man that was born?* *Job* 15. 7. Or we may read it, if we please, more exactly according to the Original, *Art thou born as the first man, or Adam, i.e.* (as the Context will shew it) art thou as understanding as the man that was *first born, viz.* as our First Parent *Adam?* By reason of this birth *Adam* is call'd *the son of God, Luk.* 3. 38. Whence the *Socinians* would gather that *Christ* hath that name upon the like account, because of his Extraordinary *Original*, because of his Miraculous *Birth*. Thus we have found that this Gentleman is ignorant of the true meaning of words in *Common Authors,* that he doth not know the acception of them in *Holy Scripture,* nay that he doth not know what his *own Authors* say, which evinces him to be triply a *Blunderer,* and

that

that he deserves no more to be call'd an *Examinator*.

Then he thinks he doth mighty things, *p.* 39. by quoting *Limborch* a very Learned Foreigner (a *System-maker* for he hath compiled a Large *System* of Divinity, though he gives it another Name; and why then doth this Gentleman talk so reproachfully of *Systems? p.* 44. *&c.*) but this his Author is a *Second Episcopius*; and therefore it was wisely done to bring him in to tell us what are the *Fundamentals* of Religion.

But it was more cunningly done in the next Paragraph to fetch in the *Sixth Article* of the *Church of England* in favour of the *Vindicator's* Conceit. Surely this his Patron, at whose feet he lays his Papers, will give him little thanks for this, for he jeers him rather than defends his Cause. Thus though they are agreed, and understand one another so far as to Impose upon the world, yet they cannot (and never will) agree to speak Truth. And indeed this Worthy Writer foresignified something of this nature. He is a *boding* sort of man, you may perceive, for thus he speaks in his Humble Dedicatory to the Vindicator, *If I have mistaken your sense, or used weak reasonings in your de-*

fence (and behold! here he doth both) *I crave your pardon.* And so you may, and I will tell you for your comfort, he will soon forgive you, for he knows that your heart is right, *i.e.* for the Good Cause, and therefore a little Mistaking of him out of weakness is pardonable.

Then he hales in *Mr. Chillingworth* by head and shoulders, *p.* 40. pronouncing him very definitively *the ablest defender of the Religion of Protestants that the Church ever had*; which is too high a Character for him, though he was a person of Great Parts and Learning. Why must he be said to be *the Ablest Defender* when we can name so many Eminent Writers in other Countreys that have perform'd this task? Or, if he means the *Church of England*, why must he have the absolute Preference to Others that we can name here, especially that Great Ornament and Glory of our Church, whom I had occasion to mention before, who hath so Learnedly defended the *Religion of Protestants?* I, but he writ against *Crellius*, and therefore he must not be the *Ablest Defender.* Again, there is a reason well known to the world why Mr. *Chillingworth* hath

the

the *Preheminence* in the opinion of this Writer and his Confederates, but of that at some other time perhaps. Let us now go on, and see what this Gentleman gets by his producing of Mr. *Chillingworth*; and it is no other than this, a plain confutation of the *Vindicator*'s Project concerning the reducing of Religion to a Point, and no more. For these are that Worthy Man's words, *The Bible, the Bible, I say the Bible only is the Religion of Protestants*. And I say so too, but this Gentleman and the Author of *the Reasonableness of Christianity* are of another opinion, for according to them it is not the *Bible*, but a very *Small Portion* of it that is the *Religion of Protestants*. They acknowledg that Some few Verses in several Chapters of the *Four Evangelists* and the *Acts* are matter of Faith or Religion, but they do not cry *the Bible, the Bible, the Bible*, they do not think that All and Every one of the Fundamental Truths in the Whole Scripture are the necessary matter of our Belief. Thus I think this Reverend Scribe might have spared the quoting of Mr. *Chillingworth*, unless he delights in confuting himself and his New Convert.

Afterwards he nibbles at some other passages in my Discourse, but flies off into Impertinencies. Only one thing I meet with that is very Remarkable, and I request the Reader to attend to it. *There are* (saith he) *some that of Deists have been reconciled to the Christian faith by the Unitarian books, and have profess'd much satisfaction therein*, p. 42. You may perceive that they are making of *Proselytes* as fast as they can, and among the rest some *Deists* come in to them, and so (as the Apostle speaks of Seducers and those that are Seduced, 2 *Pet*. 2. 20.) *the latter end is worse with them than the beginning*: for whereas before they owned a *Natural Religion*, now they become guilty of perverting and prophaning a *Revealed* one. They are so far from being *reconciled to the Christian Faith*, that they oppose and contradict it, and even defie the *Main Articles* of this Religion which is owing to Divine Revelation. Such Converts as these have no reason to *profess much satisfaction in the Unitarian books*, unless Corrupting the Christian faith be to be chosen before plain *Theism*. To speak the plain truth (and it is the design of these Papers to do so) and that which every Thinking

Opinions Confuted. 135

ing and Confidering Man cannot but difcern, the *Socinians* are but the Journeymen of the *Deists*, and they are fet on work by them, for thefe latter hope to compafs their Defign, which is to impair the Credit of the *Chriftian Religion* and of thofe *Infpired Writings* which give us an account of it, they hope (I fay) effectually to compafs this defign by the help of fuch Good Inftruments as they find the *Socianiz'd* Men to be. You fee then what ground this Gentleman hath to think that the *Deifts* are Profelytes to the *Unitarians*.

Then he proceeds to make a long harangue about the *Obfcurity of Syftematical Fundamentals*, *p*. 44. &c. but never was poor Creature fo bewildred as he is. Only he happily lights upon the *Quakers*, *p*. 44, 45. where it is worth obferving that the man doth not know his Friends from his Foes, nor thefe from them. He rails againft this fort of men (who he faith would be counted *the only People of God*) and yet it is certain that they are his brethren-*Socinians*. *They utterly difown the Scripture as the Rule of Faith*, he faith: and doth not our late *Socinian* Writer fymbolize with them when he declares that the Divine Truths con-

K 4 tained

tained in the *Epistles* of the Holy Apostles (which are a considerable part of *Scripture*) are not the Necessary matter of Faith? He complains that *the Quakers turn the Gospel into an Allegory*; but the fore mention'd Author doth much worse, for he represents the greatest Part of the Gospel-discoveries as Superfluous and Needless. In giving us the farther Character of the *Quakers*, he in lively colours represents the *Socinians*, for these are his words concerning them, *Retaining still the words wherein the Christian Faith is expressed, though in an Equivocal Sense, they have made a shift to be reputed generally Christians*. Certainly there could not be a better Pourtraiture of the *Racovian* Writers, for it is known that they are crafty and sophistical, and quote Scripture only to pervert it. They acknowledg *Christ* to be *God,* and an *Expiatory Sacrifice,* but they mean it *Equivocally* ; they quit the true *sense* of Scripture though they retain the *words*, and by reason of this latter *have made a shift* (as this Author speaks) *to pass for Christians.* These men (whatever some few *English* Writers of the *Racovian* way hold of late) exactly side with the *Quakers* in crying down of *Water-Baptism (* for so
they

Opinions Confuted. 135

they both call it in derision.) In the Grand Point of the *Trinity* they both concur, *i. e.* to reject it, witness *W. Pen's Sandy Foundation*, by which he means the doctrine of the *Blessed Trinity*. In a quibbling manner, wherein he shews both his Ignorance and Blasphemy, he thus speaks, * *If God, as the Scriptures testifie, hath never been declared or believed but as the* HOLY ONE, *then it will follow that God is not an* HOLY THREE. *Neither can this receive the least prejudice from that frequent, but impertinent distinction, that he is One in Substance, but Three in Persons or Subsistencies.* To which all *Socinus*'s followers say *Amen*. The same Gentleman derides the doctrine of *Satisfaction*, and scoffingly calls the Asserters of it † *Satisfactionists*: and who knows not that *Transylvania* agrees here with *Pensylvania?* The Man that suffer'd at *Jerusalem* is the *Socinian* as well as the *Quakers Stile*: And generally as to the main things that relate to our *Saviour*, they perfectly accord, *viz.* in making nothing of them. If *Quakerism* then be no *Christianity*, as this our Writer reports

---

* *W. Pen's Sandy Foundation. p.* 12. † *Sandy Foundat. ibid.*

ports it in the same place, then we may with much more reason conclude that *Socinianism is none.* By this it appears that *Socinus* and *Fox* are well met, and that they are very Loving Friends. But they must seem to disagree, as here in this Gentleman's Papers.

Lastly, let us see the wonderful hand of God in suffering this Unthoughtful Writer to produce *a Paper written by a Jesuite in the late Reign, entituled an Address,* &c. And in this Address, he saith, *he goes about to shew that the Scriptures commonly alledg'd for the Trinity, admit of another sense. He goes the same way in the Article of the Incarnation.* What! had he not enough of the *Quaker* but he must bring in the *Jesuite?* And must he tell the world that the *Jesuitical* Writers take the part of the *Socinians?* must he publickly give notice that they both carry on the same work, and joyntly conspire to pervert the *Scriptures* in order to it? For the credit of the Cause, it had been better to have placed this under a former head, and to have told the Reader that some *Jesuites* (as well as some *Deists*) are *Converts* to *Socinianism.* But he hath blurted it out that *Ignatius Loyola* and *Faustus Socinus* were of kin. Surely ly this Author must not be employ'd any more to write in defence of the Cause. He must be no longer a *Double-Column'd* Writer: they must look out for a man that is not so Open-hearted, one that can handle his Weapon with more Cunning, for this man hath stabb'd his own Cause.

But because this Writer in the beginning and towards the end of his Papers is pleas'd to use some words of Deference and Respect, I will not be backward to return his Civility in the same kind by letting him know that I suppose him to be a *Person of Ingenuity and Learning* (only I wish he had *shew'd* it in his late Undertaking) and that *I would not have made opposition to him in any other Points* but These which are the Foundation, Basis and Ground-work of *Christianity*, and the very Life and Soul of our *Religion*, and therefore none is to be permitted to treat them *irreverently* and *scoffingly*, as he and his Associates have lately done. But I entertain some hope that this Unsavoury *Tang* will wear off in time.

And thus I have finished both my *Replies* to the Gentlemen's Writings against me: and I have wholly confined my

self

self to these, and not ventured to guess at their Persons, or make any Reflections of that kind, for that is a thing which I abhor. Nay, though the *Vindicator* by his reflecting upon my *Degree*, *p.* 24. and 36. and *Calling*, *p.* 36, and before, *p.* 26, and before that, *p.* 9. had given me occasion to enquire into his Quality and Character, yet I purposely forbore to meddle with any such Considerations. And so as to the *Examinator*, I could easily have traced his Person and Station, and offer'd some Remarks upon either, but I made it not my business to observe Who they were that wrote, but what they had written. And it was necessary to do this latter with some Salt and Keenness, that the levity of their Arguments might be the better exposed, and that I might in a lawful and innocent way retaliate that Liberty which they had taken. And indeed the *Socinian* Gentlemen must shew themselves very Disingenuous (which I will not presume of them) if they be dissatisfied with me for my Freedom of discourse, when in all their Writings they profess to use it. And it is plain that they make use of it: for
who

who sees not that * they have been very sharp upon some of the most Eminent and Venerable Persons of our Church? They have handled the late Archbishop and some of his Reverend Brethren (who in their Writings shewed their dislike of the *Socinian* doctrines) with no excess of Respect: And they represent them and the whole Clergy as Mercenary, Timerous, and False hearted: They would perswade the world that the doctrine of the *Trinity* is defended by them merely because they are bribed or forced to it. And others of their Writers have been very severe upon the *Trinitarians* in their late Prints. And therefore with good reason some of These have been free with them again, especially that Worthy Person who undertook the Defence of the *Archbishop* and the *Bishop of Worcester*, and hath with great Vivacity and Sharpness reflected on the *Socinian* Errors, and with as great Solidity and Composedness establish'd the contrary Truths, and hath not spared that

---

* Considerations on the Explications of the doctrine of the Trinity.

that Socinian Author whom he grapples with, no not in the least. I suppose none will grudg *me* that Freedom which this Gentleman and others have taken in their *Replies* to the *Racovian* Writers, especially seeing I have not (as I conceive) made ill use of it. But of that let the Reader judg.

F I N I S.

BOOKS written by the Reverend Mr. John Edwards.

AN Enquiry into several Remakable Texts of the Old and New Testament which contain some Difficulty in them, with a Probable Resolution of them, in two Vol. 8°.

A Discourse concerning the *Authority, Stile* and *Perfection* of the Books of the Old and New Testament, with a Continued Illustration of several Difficult Texts throughout the whole Work. In three Vol. 8°.

Some Thoughts concerning the several Causes and Occasions of Atheism, especially in the Present Age, with some brief Reflections on Socinianism, and on a Late Book entituled, *The Reasonableness of Christianity as deliver'd in the Scriptures.* 8°.

A Demonstration of the *Existence* and *Providence* of God from the Contemplation of the visible Structure of the *Greater* and the *Lesser World.* In two Parts.

Parts. The first, shewing the Excellent Contrivance of the *Heavens*, *Earth*, *Sea*, &c. The second, the wonderful Formation of the Body of Man.

Socinianism Unmask'd: A Discourse shewing the Unreasonableness of a Late Writer's Opinion, concerning the Necessity of only *One Article of Christian Faith*, and of his other Assertions in his Late Book Entituled, *The Reasonableness of Christianity as deliver'd in the Scriptures*, and in his *Vindication* of it; with a brief Reply to another (Professed) Socinian Writer.

All sold by Jonathan Robinson *at the* Golden Lyon, *and* John Wyat *at the* Rose *in St.* Paul's *Church-yard.*

Titles in This Series

1

Burnet, Thomas
*Remarks Upon an Essay Concerning Humane
Understanding: in a Letter Address'd to the Author*
(London, 1697)

bound with

Locke, John
*An Answer to Remarks Upon an Essay Concerning Humane
Understanding, etc.*
(London, 1697)

bound with

Burnet, Thomas
*Second Remarks Upon an Essay Concerning Humane
Understanding, in a Letter Address'd to the Author.
Being a Vindication of the First Remarks, Against the Answer
of Mr. Locke's, at the End of His Reply to the
Lord Bishop of Worcester*
(London, 1697)

bound with

Burnet, Thomas
Third Remarks Upon an Essay Concerning Humane Understanding, in a Letter to the Author
(London, 1699)

bound with

Porter, Noah
'Marginalia Locke-a-na,' in the New Englander and Yale Review, *July, 1887, Vol. XI, pp. 33–40.*
(New Haven, 1887)

2

Collins, Anthony
An Essay Concerning the Use of Reason in Propositions, the Evidence Whereof Depends Upon Human Testimony
(London, 1707)

bound with

Collins, Anthony
A Discourse of Free-thinking, Occasion'd by the Rise and Growth of a Sect Call'd Free-thinkers
(London, 1713)

3

Dewhurst, Kenneth
John Locke, Physician and Philosopher
(London, 1963)

4

Edwards, John
Some Thoughts Concerning the Several Causes and Occasions of Atheism, Especially in the Present Age
(London, 1695)

bound with

Edwards, John
*Socinianism Unmask'd. A Discourse Shewing the
Unreasonableness of a Late Writer's Opinion Concerning the
Necessity of Only One Article of Christian Faith . . .*
(London, 1696)

5

Filmer, Sir Robert
Patriarcha and Other Political Works of Sir Robert Filmer
(Edited by Peter Laslett, Oxford, 1949)

6

King, Peter (Lord), Editor
*The Life and Letters of John Locke, with Extracts from His
Journals and Common-Place Books*
(London, 1884)

7

Lee, Henry
*Anti-Scepticism: or, Notes Upon Each Chapter of
Mr. Lock's Essay Concerning Humane Understanding*
(London, 1702)

8

Lough, John
*Locke's Travels in France, 1675–1679; As Related in His
Journals, Correspondence and Other Papers*
(Cambridge, 1953)

9

MacLean, Kenneth
John Locke and English Literature of the Eighteenth Century
(New Haven, 1936)

10

Parker, Samuel
A Demonstration of the Divine Authority of the Law of Nature, and of the Christian Religion
(London, 1681)

11

Polin, Raymond
La Politique morale de John Locke
(Paris, 1960)

12

Proast, Jonas
The Argument of the Letter Concerning Toleration, Briefly Consider'd and Answer'd
(Oxford, 1690)

bound with

Proast, Jonas
A Third Letter Concerning Toleration: in Defence of the Arguments of the Letter Concerning Toleration, Briefly Consider'd and Answer'd
(Oxford, 1691)

bound with

Proast, Jonas
A Second Letter to the Author of the Three Letters for Toleration. From the Author of the Arguments of the Letter Concerning Toleration, Briefly Consider'd and Answer'd
(Oxford, 1704)

13

Sergeant, John
Solid Philosophy Asserted, Against the Fancies of the Ideists: or, the Method to Science Farther Illustrated. With Reflexions on Mr. Locke's Essay Concerning Human Understanding
(London, 1697)

14

Tagart, Edward
Locke's Writings and Philosophy Historically Considered and Vindicated from the Charge of Contributing to the Skepticism of Hume
(London, 1855)

15

Toland, John
Christianity Not Mysterious
(London, 1696)

16

Watts, Isaac
Logick: or, the Right Use of Reason in the Enquiry After Truth, With a Variety of Rules to Guard Against Error, in the Affairs of Religion and Human Life, as Well as in the Sciences
(Second Edition, London, 1726)